Bald
Plain English

Baldrige in Plain English

Understanding Performance
Excellence

First Edition
2015–2016

John Vinyard

ASQ Quality Press
Milwaukee, Wisconsin

American Society for Quality, Quality Press, Milwaukee, WI 53203
© 2015 by ASQ
All rights reserved. Published 2015.
Printed in the United States of America.

21 20 19 18 17 16 15   5 4 3 2 1

Library of Congress Cataloging-in-Publication Data

Vinyard, John,
Baldrige in plain English: understanding performance excellence /
    John Vinyard.
ISBN 9780873899215 (soft cover: alk. paper)
LCSH: Malcolm Baldrige National Quality Award. | Total quality
    management—United States. | Organizational effectiveness. | Performance.
LCC HD62.15 .V557 2015 | DDC 658.4/013—dc23
                    2015039282

No part of this book may be reproduced in any form or by any means, electronic, mechanical, photocopying, recording, or otherwise, without the prior written permission of the publisher.

Publisher: Lynelle Korte
Acquisitions Editor: Matt T. Meinholz
Managing Editor: Paul Daniel O'Mara
Production Administrator: Randall Benson

ASQ Mission: The American Society for Quality advances individual, organizational, and community excellence worldwide through learning, quality improvement, and knowledge exchange.

Attention Bookstores, Wholesalers, Schools, and Corporations: ASQ Quality Press books, video, audio, and software are available at quantity discounts with bulk purchases for business, educational, or instructional use. For information, please contact ASQ Quality Press at 800-248-1946, or write to ASQ Quality Press, P.O. Box 3005, Milwaukee, WI 53201-3005.

To place orders or to request ASQ membership information, call 800-248-1946. Visit our Web site at www.asq.org/quality-press.

∞ Printed on acid-free paper

Quality Press
600 N. Plankinton Ave.
Milwaukee, WI 53203-2914
E-mail: authors@asq.org

The Global Voice of Quality®

Dedication

*This book is dedicated to my Wife, JoAnn Olson Vinyard
One of my great joys in life is discussing almost any topic with her.
She, however, frequently, asks me to "Put it in Plain English."*

When she read this dedication her response was:

*"I frequently tell you the secrets of the universe,
and you ask me to 'Put it in Plain English.'"*

Table of Contents

Dedication v

Acknowledgements ix

About the Author xi

Preface... xiii

Organizational Profile
    Organizational Description (P.1) 1
    Organizational Situation (P.2) 11

Category 1—Leadership
    Senior Leadership (1.1) 21
    Governance and Societal Responsibilities (1.2) 30

Category 2—Strategy
    Strategy Development (2.1) 41
    Strategy Implementation (2.2) 51

Category 3—Customer
    Voice of the Customer (3.1) 57
    Customer Engagement (3.2) 64

Category 4—Measurement, Analysis, and Knowledge Management
    Measurement, Analysis and Improvement of
        Organizational Performance (4.1) 73
    Knowledge Management, Information
        and Information Technology (4.2) 82

Category 5—Workforce
　　Workforce Environment (5.1) 89
　　Workforce Engagement (5.2) 94

Category 6—Operations
　　Work Processes (6.1) 105
　　Operational Effectiveness (6.2) 114

Category 7—Results
　　Product and Process Results (7.1) 121
　　Customer-Focused Results (7.2) 127
　　Workforce-Focused Results (7.3) 130
　　Leadership and Governance Results (7.4) 132
　　Financial and Market Results (7.5) 137

Glossary of Key Terms 141

Index 167

Acknowledgements

The Malcolm Baldrige National Quality Award (Baldrige) began with a dream in the mid-1980s, which ultimately resulted in legislation in 1987. Baldrige was designed to make U.S. organizations more competitive, but its impact has been worldwide.

Putting a book like this together reminds me of all the people who have really made a difference. This list of contributors starts with Curt Reimann, Harry Hertz, Bob Fangmeyer, and the entire Baldrige Team. These are some of the most professional and dedicated employees in our country. They are making a difference to our lives, our nation, and the quality of life for employees worldwide. The Baldrige Team is helping to improve our nation in a manner that will impact our children and grandchildren. These words were true when there were 40 staff members. It's even more true now when there are only 20 staff. Thank you.

Organizations that have embraced, and are using, the Criteria for Performance Excellence are more competitive in the marketplace, and are better places to work. Those of us who have been fortunate enough to have worked closely with the NIST Baldrige Team have benefited every day from that association. Not only are they gifted professionals, but they tirelessly share their knowledge and experience to help others. They are always there for help or advice. I feel privileged to be their friend.

The use of this model is pivotal to organizational performance. At a time when many organizations want a handout from the government, I have not heard about any of those wanting a handout who are focused on the 11 core values of Baldrige, or who are using this model to try to turn their organizations around. I hope they see the value of the processes which Baldrige helps an organization to define, and the improved metrics those processes drive. That insight would help our nation and the world.

I also thank my office support staff—Jane Sonnet and Megan Jordan.

Last, but certainly not least, I thank my wife JoAnn whose love and support has been pivotal.

As with any list of acknowledgements, I know my list runs the risk of not mentioning someone who has been key to the development of my thoughts. In that vein, I thank all those who have worked with me over the years and who have shared their lessons, learning, knowledge, and wisdom. I feel those clients, coworkers, and friends are some of the most talented individuals in the world, and they are generous with their wisdom. Thank you, from my heart! I could not have written this without your excellence, your attitude of sharing, your friendship, and your help.

About the Author
John Vinyard

John is the managing partner and co-founder of Genitect, an organizational diagnosis, design, and transformation firm with offices in Atlanta and New York.

John has worked with numerous clients in the United States and international firms in Europe, the Middle East, India, Asia, and the Pacific Rim. He specializes in working with leadership teams to help transform their organizations. He has worked with 15 Baldrige recipients during their journey (and more than 50 state and other award recipients), helping them use the Baldrige Model to significantly impact their competitiveness and bottom-line results.

John is licensed by the Federal Aviation Administration (FAA) in Airframe and Powerplant Maintenance (A&P License).

John is on the Board of Directors of Navicent Health, Macon, Georgia.

Preface

Introduction

The *Baldrige Criteria for Performance Excellence (CPE)* model was created by Public Law 100-107, the Malcolm Baldrige National Quality Improvement Act, signed by President Reagan on August 20, 1987. The purpose of the legislation is to help improve the quality and productivity of American companies by promoting an awareness of performance excellence as an increasingly vital element in achieving a competitive edge.

Millions of copies of the Criteria have been distributed, and over 1500 organizations have applied for recognition at the national level since the award was created. Additionally, many thousands of organizations have applied for their local or state awards as a stepping-stone to applying for the award at the national level.

The award is managed by the Malcolm Baldrige National Quality Award (MBNQA) Office, under the National Institute of Standards and Technology (NIST), within the Department of Commerce.

The use of the CPE to improve performance has increased worldwide. This has not only spread to additional sectors, such as education, healthcare, non-profit, and government organizations, but also has spread around the world. According to NIST, there are 49 active CPE-based award programs in 41 states in the United States. A lead state program helps those states not covered by an award. In addition, approximately 79 award programs are located across the world. For example, in addition to the Deming Prize, there is a CPE-based award in Japan. Elements of the CPE are also used in the European Quality Award (EFQM) and Canadian Awards for Excellence (NIST, 2004 Presentation). Given the growth in both the types of organizations and the geography, we conclude that the CPE has truly become a global benchmark, and the CPE has become accepted as a worldwide standard for performance excellence.

For example, some of the fastest growing, most profitable, and largest companies in India are using the CPE as their basis for improvement.

In some corporations, it is so pervasive that, if some of their division CEOs cannot score well on this scale, they are no longer allowed to use the corporate identity!

The definition of success for organizations of all types (profit seeking, non-profit, and government) is continuously changing and becoming increasingly complex. From the mid-1940s to the 1970s, the limited global competition allowed business leaders in the United States to focus mainly on financial results. The "party" ended sometime around 1980 when Xerox woke up to a situation where the Japanese were selling copiers in the United States for what it was costing Xerox to make them (Kotter & Heskett, 1992).

During the 1980s, quality became a key success factor and was directly linked to market and ultimately financial success. In the beginning, many proposed that producing high quality was simply too expensive. However, organizations eventually discovered that high quality resulted in reduced cost and increased market share. As the service industry and the knowledge worker industries in particular increased in size and importance, leaders discovered that talented, passionate people are also a key to high quality and financial performance.

During the 1990s successful organizations became quite good at "connecting the dots" or as FedEx called it—"people, service, profit" (AMA, 1991). The bar is being raised once again to include sustainable results in three key areas: financial, environmental, and societal, or as Elkington, Emerson, and Beloe (2006) call it—the triple bottom line.

Clearly, financial results alone are not enough to ensure a successful and sustainable organization. This is one of the reasons the holistic view of an organization, as represented by Baldrige, is attractive to these visionary organizations.

The CPE framework provides a high-level or *Category* view of the holistic nature of the CPE. Seven categories are shown in the diagram. Within these seven categories and the Organizational Profile there are 42 areas to address. There are five areas to address in the Organizational Profile, 29 areas to address in the first six process categories and finally eight areas to address in the results category.

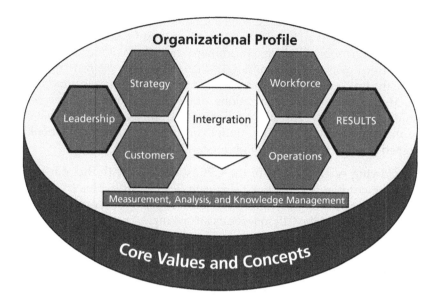

Figure 1.2 The CPE Framework
Source: NIST (2015–2016, p. 1)

For the convenience of the reader, the actual CPE (Baldrige) Criteria questions are presented verbatim in the following format:

❓ The Criteria For Performance Excellence (CPE)

> **CPE Questions**—*The actual Malcolm Baldrige National Quality Award Criteria for Performance Excellence (CPE) is presented verbatim. Included are the actual questions and notes (explanations) from the CPE.*
>
> This is provided through the courtesy of:
>
> - The Baldrige Performance Excellence Program, National Institute of Standards and Technology (NIST), United States Department of Commerce, January 2015, Criteria for Performance Excellence, Gaithersburg, MD.

Reading the criteria can be challenging; many people have difficulty understanding what all the elements mean on their first (or 10th?) reading. For those who become Baldrige Examiners, the criteria often "come alive" in their third year as an examiner. In that third year, the flow becomes clearer, the linkages make more sense, and the overall process is more evident. Many people and organizations, however, do not have three years to study and wait. Organizations entering this process need tools that can help them understand the CPE model and process quickly. This book is designed to make the process of understanding the CPE easier.

Following each selection of the CPE is a section with that particular part of the criteria described as *Baldrige in Plain English*. This is an introduction to the basics of that particular area. It provides a common sense description of what the CPE questions are asking.

Baldrige in Plain English— With the Name of the Criteria Section

This is written as a *foundation* for understanding the Baldrige Criteria—hence the brick wall.

Following the Criteria, each section includes an introduction to the basics of the *Area to Address*. This is a common sense description of what the CPE in the particular *Area to Address* is trying to achieve. This explanation focuses on what the CPE actually means and what some organizations do; not just the questions in the CPE.

The focus is designed to help new and experienced users gain a better understanding of the CPE, the background, as well as the meaning.

This book is a companion document with:

The Baldrige Users Guide

And

Baldrige For Leaders

All of these are published by ASQ Quality Press.

Organizational Profile

P.1 *Organizational Description*

P.1a ORGANIZATIONAL ENVIRONMENT

> *Culture is what is left after everything we have learned has been forgotten. It consists of a deepened understanding, a breadth of outlook, an unbiased approach, and a heart that has deep sympathy and strength of courage.*
>
> G. BROMLEY OXNAM

The Criteria For Performance Excellence (CPE)

In your response, answer the following questions:

a. Organizational Environment

1. **Product Offerings:** What are your main product offerings? (See the note on the next page.) What is the relative importance of each to your success? What mechanisms do you use to deliver your products?

2. **Mission, Vision, and Values:** What are your stated mission, vision, and values? What are your organization's core competencies, and what is their relationship to your mission?

3. **Workforce Profile:** What is your workforce profile? What recent changes have you experienced in workforce composition or your workforce needs? What are:

- Your workforce or employee groups and segments?
- The educational requirements for different employee groups and segments?
- The key drivers that engage them in achieving your mission and vision?

What are your organized bargaining units (union representation)? What are your organization's special health and safety requirements?

4. **Assets:** What are your major facilities, technologies, and equipment?

5. **Regulatory Requirements:** What is the regulatory environment under which you operate? What are the applicable occupational health and safety regulations; accreditation, certification, or registration requirements; industry standards; and environmental, financial, and product regulations?

Notes:

P. Your responses to the Organizational Profile questions are very important. They set the context for understanding your organization and how it operates. Your responses to all other questions in the Baldrige Criteria should relate to the organizational context you describe in this Profile. Your responses to the Organizational Profile questions allow you to tailor your responses to all other questions to your organization's unique needs.

P.1a(1). Product offerings and products are the goods and services you offer in the marketplace. Mechanisms for delivering products to your end-use customers might be direct or might be indirect, through dealers, distributors, collaborators, or channel partners. *Nonprofit organizations might refer to their product offerings as programs, projects, or services.*

P.1a(2). Core competencies are your organization's areas of greatest expertise. They are those strategically important capabilities that are central to fulfilling your mission or that provide an advantage in your marketplace or service environment. Core competencies are frequently challenging for competitors or suppliers and partners to imitate and frequently preserve your competitive advantage.

P.1a(2). Core competencies are one example of concepts that are woven throughout the Criteria to ensure a systems approach to organizational performance management. Other such concepts include innovation, use of data and information to review performance and create knowledge, and change readiness and management.

P.1a(3). Workforce or employee groups and segments (including organized bargaining units) might be based on type of employment or contract-reporting relationship, location (including telework), tour of duty, work environment, use of certain family-friendly policies, or other factors.

P.1a(3). Organizations that also rely on volunteers and unpaid interns to accomplish their work should include these groups as part of their workforce.

P.1a(5). Industry standards might include industrywide codes of conduct and policy guidance. In the Criteria, industry refers to the sector in which you operate. *For nonprofit organizations, this sector might be charitable organizations, professional associations and societies, religious organizations, or government entities—or a subsector of one of these.* Depending on the regions in which you operate, environmental regulations might include greenhouse gas emissions, carbon regulations and trading, and energy efficiency.

NIST (2015–2016) pp. 4–5

Baldrige in Plain English— Organizational Environment

The *Organizational Environment* portion of the Organizational Profile is focused on the internal aspects of the organization, including: key offerings (products and services); organizational culture; people; major technologies, equipment, and facilities; and the regulatory environment that the organization must operate within. The first question typically asks what the organization produces (for example products and services). In the Criteria for Performance Excellence, NIST changed the definition of products: "'product offerings' and 'products' refer to the goods and services that your organization offers in the marketplace. Mechanisms for product delivery to your end-use customers might be direct or through dealers, distributors, collaborators, or channel partners. Nonprofit organizations might refer to their product offerings as programs, projects, or services." In many places in this book, the terms "products and services" are still used to remind the user that it is not just the products that are being addressed. Subsequent questions ask for a description of the internal characteristics of the organization. These descriptions will be used later to assess whether the organization is focusing on the most important aspects of their internal environment. For example, if there are several employee groups, and one is in a nationwide shortage, the organization would be expected to take action to attract and retain employees in that particular group.

Product Offerings

Sometimes the identification of the products, services, and operations is easy and straightforward, and sometimes it's not. For example, for the local coffee shop entrepreneur, some might say that coffee is the central product, while others might say that a forum for the exchange of information is the primary product or service, and coffee is simply an enhancer. If the primary product is the latter, the coffee shop might offer free wireless Internet along with a variety of coffees and snacks. How these products and services are delivered is another decision. This portion of the Criteria also asks about the delivery mechanisms. How the products are delivered may have a significant impact on most of the organization's actions, including communication, planning, deployment, measures, improvement cycles, and other actions. For the local coffee shop, delivery might be in the form of counter service, a drive-up window, and maybe even Internet ordering and mail delivery for coffee beans and accessories.

One of the key questions asked in this area is "the relative importance of each to your success" (NIST, 2015–2016, p.4). Without understanding the importance of each product and service (both now and in the future), an organization cannot make the right decisions, take the right risks, and may not succeed.

Vision and Mission

The culture of the organization is a critical enabler to the organization's direction and internal environment. If the culture is characterized by an open, collaborative, and creative operating style, and is known for its innovation, then detailed procedures on information sharing might not fit. For example, at the local coffee shop, the desired environment may require a culture of teamwork focused on creating an atmosphere for information exchange, a place where as a customer, "everybody knows your name."

The culture and purpose of the organization, along with its vision and values, help establish the areas of greatest importance to the organization's success. Consider ownership, for example. If the owners are the same as the customers, the central purpose of the organization may be different than if the owners are investors in a for-profit company. In this example, the cooperative type organization (where owners are customers) is typically focused on the greatest benefit to the members at the least expense.

The *Mission* is the overall function of the organization, the *Vision* is the desired future state, and the *Values* are the guiding principles. Most organizations have lofty beliefs and values. The key, however, is the ability to turn these beliefs and values into actions and behaviors. To do this, some organizations have taken the values and translated them into behaviors that are expected of every employee in every transaction with every stakeholder. More advanced organizations have even taken the behaviors and expanded the definition of them to include behaviors that are not acceptable, and how you can recover if you demonstrate one of the unacceptable behaviors. Recovery from some behaviors, such as a breach of integrity, may not be possible.

The organization should also be clear on its *Core Competency* (ies) and the relationship to the Mission. Beyond this basic linkage, the organization should also be able to link the Core Competencies to the *Success Factors, Strategic Challenges, Strategic Objectives, Strategic Advantages, Metrics Tracked*, and the *Action Plans*. See the Glossary for the definition of each of these terms.

Workforce Profile

Now that we know what work is to be accomplished, as well as the culture (beliefs, norms, values, behaviors, and symbols) needed to accomplish it, who is going to do the work? What type of employees does the organization use to accomplish the work? What is the breakdown of the knowledge, skills, and abilities required of the workforce? The employee demographics will impact the types and methods of measurement needed to acquire, develop, utilize, evaluate, and promote the workforce that is uniquely suited to the business. These demographics form the employee profile. However, the same types of employees in different work environments may have different requirements and may need to be classified differently. For example, a secretary in an office environment will have different safety requirements than a secretary in a factory. Also, we can control the work environment for a nurse in a hospital, but we may not be able to control the work environment for a home-care nurse.

For the local coffee shop, the workforce might consist of supervisors who are full-time employees, and workers who are part-time employees and full-time students. The bigger question, of course, is what these two groups of employees need to be successful. In each case, the organization needs to understand the requirements for each position and employee group, so the steps necessary to meet those requirements can be included in the organization's plans.

Assets

After the work, the culture, and the employees are determined, the next question is, "Where are we going to do the work, and what kind of equipment do you need?" Specifically, what are the organization's major technologies, equipment, and facilities—Assets? This will influence what is important to measure, how best to measure it, and how best to aggregate the data. The answer to this question, of course, varies widely depending on the type of business. A Fortune 100 "high tech" firm with operations around the world will have a very different answer to this question than the local coffee shop. The local coffee shop may only need a shop with furniture, some coffee-making equipment, and high-speed wireless Internet.

Regulatory Requirements

The last element of the organizational environment is the regulatory environment. What external rules and regulations does the organization have to comply with in order to do business? The regulatory environment is a key variable to understanding the most important measures in anticipating issues and preventing problems with areas of public well-being. This element, of course, is again very different for a nuclear power plant than it is for the local coffee shop down the street.

Most organizations are regulated by financial (IRS) and environmental (EPA) agencies, but it is also important to understand the regulatory agencies unique to the organization's industry. For example, a hospital is regulated by numerous groups and agencies that would not be important to an aerospace firm. Conversely, an aerospace firm may be regulated by Federal Aviation Administration (FAA) laws and regulations that would not apply to the hospital. Once again, these agencies are important because the training, measures, goals, objectives, and actions should address the regulatory environment. The organization should seek to meet or exceed all regulations applicable to their operations.

P.1b ORGANIZATIONAL RELATIONSHIPS

The price of greatness is responsibility.

WINSTON CHURCHILL

The Criteria For Performance Excellence (CPE)

> In your response, answer the following questions:
>
> b. Organizational Relationships
>
> 1. **Organizational Structure:** What are your organizational structure and governance system? What are the reporting relationships among your governance board, senior leaders, and parent organization, as appropriate?
>
> 2. **Customers and Stakeholders:** What are your key market segments, customer groups, and stakeholder groups, as appropriate? What are their key requirements and expectations of your products, customer support services, and operations? What are the differences in these requirements and expectations among market segments, customer groups, and stakeholder groups?
>
> 3. **Suppliers and Partners:** What are your key types of suppliers, partners, and collaborators? What role do they play:
>
>   - In your work systems, especially in producing and delivering your key products and customer support services?
>
>   - In enhancing your competitiveness?
>
>   What are your key mechanisms for two-way communication with suppliers, partners, and collaborators? What role, if any, do these organizations play in contributing and implementing innovations in your organization? What are your key supply chain requirements?

Notes:

P.1b(1). *For some nonprofit organizations, governance and reporting relationships might include relationships with major funding sources, such as granting agencies or foundations.*

P.1b(2). Customers include the users and potential users of your products. *For some nonprofit organizations, customers might include members, taxpayers, citizens, recipients, clients, and beneficiaries, and market segments might be referred to as constituencies.*

P.1b(2). Customer groups might be based on common expectations, behaviors, preferences, or profiles. Within a group, there may be customer segments based on differences and commonalities. You might subdivide your market into market segments based on product lines or features, distribution channels, business volume, geography, or other factors that you use to define a market segment.

P.1b(2). The requirements of your customer groups and market segments might include on-time delivery, low defect levels, safety, security, ongoing price reductions, the leveraging of technology, rapid response, after-sales service, and multilingual services. The requirements of your stakeholder groups might include socially responsible behavior and community service. *For some nonprofit organizations, these requirements might also include administrative cost reductions, at-home services, and rapid response to emergencies.*

P.1b(3). Communication mechanisms should be two-way and use understandable language. They might involve in-person contact, e-mail, social media, or the telephone. For many organizations, these mechanisms may change as marketplace, customer, or stakeholder requirements change.

NIST (2015–2016) pp. 4–5

 Baldrige in Plain English— Organizational Relationships

With the internal environmental context of the organization established in (P.1a), the key relationships that impact the internal operations of the organization (P.1b) are reviewed.

Organizational Structure

The first question asks about the organizational structure and governance system. More specifically, what are the reporting relationships among the board of directors, senior leaders, and parent organization (if there is one)? Who are these people, what do they want, and how does the organization interact with them? The answer to this question varies widely depending on size of the organization, ownership structure, and the level of autonomy of the organization. For example, a single owner Limited Liability Company will have a very different board of directors than a publicly traded corporation.

Note: this area is an opportunity to clearly describe a number of aspects of the organization, including:

- The organization structure (chain of command)
- The relationships with other key groups (such as Nursing Shared Governance Councils or Medical Committees in Health Care)
- The parent organization (including key committees and shared services, as appropriate)
- Although it is not specifically asked for in the Criteria, this is a good place to describe other factors which can help to understand the organization such as:
  - Membership in key committees that are referenced in the application
  - Membership in key governing or leadership groups
  - Level of education or commitment of the leaders in the Baldrige Journey:
    - » Leaders trained in Performance Excellence (as a side note, it is always interesting to assess an organization on Performance Excellence when its leaders have had little or no formal experience with the Criteria, processes, systems, or practices)

Customers and Stakeholders

Key customer segments or groups are the second type of external relationships. These groups are typically determined by the differences in customer requirements. In other words, each segment should have different needs, wants, and desires. The organization, therefore, prioritizes its needs, wants, and desires differently for each segment. For example, the local coffee shop might have several schemes for segmenting customers, including the "on-the-way-to-work" crowd, the traditional conversation crowd, and the technology crowd. The first two segments might not rate the wireless Internet as important to their experience, but the technology crowd probably would. The traditional conversation crowd might not rate speed of service as important, but the "on-the-way-to-work" crowd probably would. Thus, each segment may drink coffee and have similar coffee requirements (temperature, taste, etc.), but may have very different "experience" requirements. The processes used to segment customers should be described in item 3.2. The requirements for each segment shown in this area should be reflected in the results reported in Area to Address 7.1a. This is particularly true for Health Care applicants, many of which focus only on their clinical results in item 7.1, and do not report against the customer's requirements. The customer satisfaction, dissatisfaction, and loyalty for each segment should be reported in item 7.2.

Some organizations segment their customers by their profitability or contribution to margin. For example, airlines often classify customers into cheap-fare infrequent, leisure flyers; full-fare business flyers; and frequent flyers at various fares—the relationship mechanisms differ for each segment. Access to information, seating, etc. varies with the status of the customer. The airlines spend less time impressing the infrequent super-saver passenger than they do the frequent business passenger. This strategy is simply a matter of allocating limited resources to areas having the greatest impact on the top line in a highly competitive environment. Service levels are appropriate for the price the consumer is willing to pay. Infrequent leisure travelers are generally not loyal to a particular airline; however, business travelers who are members of clubs and benefit from status, etc., are often loyal to a particular airline.

Suppliers and Partners

Finally, suppliers are key to the quality of any organization's value chain. An old computer programmer saying warns, "Garbage in, garbage out." If our suppliers do not provide quality products and services, then most organizations will not be able to provide excellence to their customers. An old supply chain saying warns, "We no longer compete company-to-company; we compete supply chain-to-supply chain."

What roles do suppliers and distributors play in your value-creation processes? This contribution to your success will be different for virtually every organization. Nevertheless, the effective integration of the supply chain into an organization's integrated value chain is critical in today's marketplace. For example, in a coffee shop you can make lousy coffee from good beans, but you cannot make good coffee from lousy beans. In addition, if the Internet works only half the time then the experience for the technology crowd will suffer. Finally, how do you build relationships and communicate with customers and suppliers?

Supplier partners will be important to almost every organization in the next decade or so. As organizations excel at focusing on their core competencies, they will increase their outsourcing of other functions. The need for relationship management with key suppliers, partners, and collaborators will grow. It is difficult, however, to successfully outsource key operations using the traditional us vs. them procurement processes and relationship techniques.

The future of the integrated supply chain network will require close relationships and increased sharing of information. The scope and magnitude of your supplier, partner, and collaborator network will determine what is necessary to measure and how it can be used to improve performance of the entire supply chain system.

P.2 Organizational Situation

P.2a COMPETITIVE ENVIRONMENT

> *There is a tendency among some businesses to criticize and belittle their competitors. This is a bad procedure. Praise them. Learn from them. There are times when you can co-operate with them to their advantage and to yours! Speak well of them and they will speak well of you. You can't destroy good ideas. Take advantage of them.*
>
> GEORGE MATTHEW ADAMS

The Criteria For Performance Excellence (CPE)

In your response, answer the following questions:

a. Competitive Environment

1. **Competitive Position:** What is your competitive position? What are your relative size and growth in your industry or the markets you serve? How many and what types of competitors do you have?

2. **Competitiveness Changes:** What key changes, if any, are affecting your competitive situation, including changes that create opportunities for innovation and collaboration, as appropriate?

3. **Comparative Data:** What key sources of comparative and competitive data are available from within your industry? What key sources of comparative data are available from outside your industry? What limitations, if any, affect your ability to obtain or use these data?

Notes:

P.2a. Like for-profit businesses, nonprofit organizations are frequently in a highly competitive environment. Nonprofit organizations must often compete with other organizations and alternative sources of similar services to secure financial and volunteer resources, membership, visibility in appropriate communities, and media attention.

NIST (2015–2016) p. 6

 Baldrige in Plain English— Competitive Environment

The first two Areas to Address (in P.1) of the Organizational Profile focused on the organization itself—the Organizational Description, and those the organization directly interfaces with such as customers, suppliers, and partners. The remaining three Areas to Address (in P.2) in the Organizational Profile focus on the various aspects of the external environment in which the organization operates, and the methods used to continuously learn and improve to meet the challenges of that environment—the Organizational Situation.

Competitive Position

This begins with the organization's standing in relation to their competitors. Who are its competitors? How fast is the market and industry growing? What success factors will determine who wins in the marketplace? How are the organization and the competitors doing against these key success factors? How does the organization know?

Our experience has shown us that these are critical questions that are applicable to all organizations, even not-for-profit or governmental organizations. Even these organizations can be hurt competitively if they do not keep pace with the changes in the competition or changes in the products and services.

Why are these questions important? In the for-profit free marketplace, the answers to these questions are critical when developing strategies to ensure continued success and sustainable results. For example, the local coffee shop's position might be head-to-head competition with the local Starbucks. When Starbucks came to town, however, the customers loyal to the local coffee shop put bumper stickers on their cars that read "Friends don't let friends drink Starbucks." While Starbucks might make a fine cup of coffee, something else was at work here. The *free* wireless Internet at the local shop might have had something to do with it, but there were clearly other factors, including personal relationships between the customers and the owner of the local coffee shop. The good news may be that both coffee shops are thriving, perhaps because they serve different markets or customer groups. Each of them is focused on its particular product and service offerings and it is not trying to beat the other at their own game. A key question is how would each coffee shop know how it was doing against each other?

Years ago I worked with Boeing in Ft. Walton Beach, Florida. One of the history books about the region told the story of two movie theatres in town who were arch rivals. The owner of one theatre always ensured his son was first in line to buy a ticket at the competitor's theatre every morning. In the evening his son would run across town to buy the last ticket of the day. His dad would look at the two ticket numbers, and calculate (through a sophisticated analysis technique called *subtraction* using the serial numbers on the tickets) how many customers his competitor had attracted that day. Nevertheless, some more sophisticated businesses don't even do this level of reconnaissance of their competitors. How can they make valid decisions if they don't know what their competitors are doing?

Competitiveness Changes

Once the competitive position is understood, the next understanding that is reviewed is critical. In previous years, the Criteria asked "What are the principal factors that determine your success relative to your competitors?" These were called *Success Factors*.

We recommend that organizations do not lose sight of the Success Factors for their industry. In these few words, a question is asked that very few organizations can really answer: What are the few things that drive your competitive advantage? These are the things anybody in your industry needs to be good at in order to succeed. The organization should benchmark the organizations that are the best at these things. These are the things the organization should invest in improving and these are the things leaders should consider as the *lifeline* of the organization. This need to understand what is critical to your success is also true in Not-For-Profit. For example, one of our clients stores 500,000 part numbers and processes thousands of shipments each week. They *must* be good at: 1) record accuracy, 2) storage discipline, 3) preparing orders for shipment, and 4) partnering with shipping and freight forwarding organizations. If they are not good at one of these things, nothing else can make up for that shortcoming. Although this has been taken out of the Criteria, we think it is still be a critical question and can be very beneficial in helping an organization determine their strategic advantages.

The Criteria now asks about the key changes taking place that affect your competitiveness. Again, it can help an organization to determine the industry's principal factors that determine success as a step toward determining the changes taking place and/or the opportunities for innovation and collaboration to favorably impact your competitiveness.

Comparative Data

Performance measures and competitive comparisons provide evidence to increase the understanding of the competitive environment. Today's competitive environment requires advanced customer knowledge and understanding. It is one thing to understand the customers' stated wants and needs and it is quite another to understand what drives their behavior and what they will actually pay for. If the organization understands what drives its customer's behavior better than the competitors, and it aligns the organization's processes to address that behavior, it will often win in the marketplace.

Performance measures can certainly be influenced by competitors. These are some of the areas of greatest importance for comparison. Comparison measures can provide a relative measure for comparing performance levels and trends. Comparisons help organizations and their leaders to understand gaps in performance and the magnitude of these gaps. They also help the organization to set realistic but meaningful targets.

The danger in comparisons is that they can limit the organization's improvement efforts to continuously *catch up*, rather than leap beyond its competitors with innovative products, services, and processes. This is the comparison trap. Jim Collins warns that comparison is "the cardinal sin of modern life. It traps us in a game that we can't win. Once we define ourselves in terms of others, we lose the freedom to shape our own lives." Organizations are no different. Apple Inc. doesn't win in the marketplace because it is chasing its competitors' products and services. It wins by carving its own unique path and leading in the marketplace. Comparisons can help to drive an increased sense of urgency, but they need to be tempered with an understanding of the rate of change required to be a leader.

A competitive environment can be critical to future survival. It certainly will impact whether an organization merely *survives* or *thrives* in the future. Tang and Bauer, in their book *Competitive Dominance,* identify several competitive positions from "dead" to "follower" to "dominance." Knowledge of the competition and its performance, particularly through the customers' eyes, is key to developing strategies to overtake the competitor's position and dominate the market.

P.2b STRATEGIC CONTEXT

> *There are two ways of meeting difficulties: you alter the difficulties, or you alter yourself to meet them.*
>
> PHYLLIS BOTTOME

 The Criteria For Performance Excellence (CPE)

In your response, include answers to the following questions:

b. Strategic Context

What are your key strategic challenges and advantages in the areas of business, operations, societal responsibilities, and workforce?

Notes:

P.2b. Strategic challenges and advantages might relate to technology, products, finances, operations, organizational structure and culture, your parent organization's capabilities, customers and markets, brand recognition and reputation, your industry, globalization, climate change, your value chain, and people. Strategic advantages might include differentiators such as price leadership, design services, innovation rate, geographic proximity, accessibility, and warranty and product options. *For some nonprofit organizations, differentiators might also include relative influence with decision makers, ratio of administrative costs to programmatic contributions, reputation for program or service delivery, and wait times for service.*

> **P.2b.** *Throughout the Criteria*, business *refers to a nonprofit organization's main mission area or enterprise activity.*
>
> NIST (2015–2016) p. 6

Baldrige in Plain English— Strategic Context

The strategic challenges focus on four main areas: 1) business challenges and advantages; 2) operational challenges and advantages; 3) societal responsibility challenges and advantages, and 4) workforce challenges and advantages. Strategic challenges are those things coming at the organization from the outside, which the organization does not control. The organization, however, must take internal action (normally through the strategic objectives and the associated action plans) to address these challenges if the organization is to remain competitive and sustainable. This is even true for nonprofit organizations. *Not-for-profit is a tax status, not a business model!* The strategic advantages are the areas where the organization has a competitive advantage, and the factors that drive the competitive advantage are typically in the organizational objectives and are continuously strengthened and reviewed.

Business Challenges

Business challenges vary depending on the nature of the organization (for profit, nonprofit, government, etc.), but they often include how to keep black ink on the books! For example, local coffee shops are not the most highly capitalized firms in the country. Consequently, the business challenges are often focused on how to keep the cash flowing.

Operations Challenges

Operational challenges, on the other hand, generally focus on the organization's ability to meet the demands of the customers while efficiently and safely meeting or exceeding regulatory requirements. This challenge can get even more complicated when there are multiple customer groups with a range of needs or demands. For example, at the coffee shop, satisfying the demands of the on-the-way-to-work crowd might be difficult when the line is also filled with other customer groups, such as the group that lingers for conversation and often orders food to go with their coffee.

Societal Responsibility Challenges

Societal responsibility challenges address the needs of the community (which can be defined as local, state, or national). For most organizations, these change frequently. Some of the changes are optional (supporting a local program), while others may be broader in scope and mandatory (nationally mandated programs).

Workforce Challenges

Finally, there are human resource challenges. These can be at the heart of what can make an organization thrive or struggle. For example, with a coffee shop, how does it keep well-trained, motivated employees when the industry pay is relatively low and student workers graduate and create turnover on a regular basis?

Competitive Advantages

These are the things that the organization has been given, or has created, which provides them an advantage in the competitive marketplace. This advantage could be internally with their cost, schedule, or quality, or externally with their customer's perception of their value. For example, the local coffee shop had a geographic advantage before Starbucks moved to the neighborhood. No nearby competitor sold top-quality coffee. Once the geographic advantage was gone, the leaders of the coffee shop needed to understand what else would drive the customer's behavior. That advantage (or differentiator) could be either products or services, but must be something that was valued by the customer.

P.2c PERFORMANCE IMPROVEMENT SYSTEM

> *There isn't a plant or business on earth that couldn't stand a few improvements—and be better for them. Someone is going to think of them. Why not beat the other fellow to it?*
>
> ROGER B. BABSON

The Criteria For Performance Excellence (CPE)

> In your response, include answers to the following questions:
>
> c. Performance Improvement System
>
> What are the key elements of your performance improvement system, including your processes for evaluation and improvement of key organizational projects and processes?
>
> **Notes:**
>
> **P.2c.** The Baldrige Scoring System (pages 30–35 in the Baldrige Criteria) uses performance improvement through learning and integration as a dimension in assessing the maturity of organizational approaches and their deployment. This question is intended to set an overall context for your approach to performance improvement. The approach you use should be related to your organization's needs. Approaches that are compatible with the overarching systems approach provided by the Baldrige framework might include implementing a Lean Enterprise System, applying Six Sigma methodology, using Plan-Do-Check-Act (PDCA) methodology, using standards from ISO (for example 9000 or 14000), using decision science, or employing other improvement tools.
>
> NIST (2015–2016) p. 6

Baldrige in Plain English— Performance Improvement System

Performance Improvement System

This Area to Address focuses on the continuous improvement processes that are used throughout the organization. How does the organization systematically and continuously improve and stay current with the changing needs of the key stakeholders? When we boil down the essence of most of the approaches to improvement, we find that they all follow the scientific method proposed by Shewhart, and later refined by Deming. The method includes four main steps or phases: Plan, Do, Study, Act

(PDSA). The "study" step at one time was referred to as "check" (PDCA). This step, however, was changed by Deming to "study" to better reflect the meaning of the step, which is to study the results and learn from them as a basis for further action. Examples of applications of the PDSA cycle can include:

- Leadership system
- Strategy development and deployment
- Organization transformation (Baldrige assessment and improvement)
- Process improvement (continuous process improvement, Six Sigma, lean, etc.).

These approaches, in order to create sustainable change, must incorporate culture, individual, and information improvement, as needed. Any one of these without the others will not result in change that is lasting.

The improvement approach selected needs to be one that is used throughout the organization. Although the Criteria do not ask for a *specific* type of improvement approach (such as Plan-Do-Study-Act), the examiners typically expect to understand what approach is used and why. It is reasonable to use different approaches for different applications, but the reasons why each approach is used should be clear. Once the improvement approach or technique is understood, the Criteria specifically ask for the process used to maintain an overall focus on performance improvement.

- Note: Area to Address P.2c asks how the organization improves. Many responses make one of two mistakes. Either they describe improvement at such a high level that the reader cannot understand what the organization *specifically* does, or they list so many different types of improvement tools that the reader is confused as to what is used, when, and why.

It's key that performance improvement is used throughout any organization. It does not bode well for an organization if it is proud that it adopted a trendy technique early, has trained everybody, and nobody is using the technique. Everybody should be using the improvement techniques endorsed by the organization, not just a few employees.

Category 1—Leadership

1.1 *Senior Leadership*

1.1a VISION, VALUES, AND MISSION

> *As soon as a man climbs to a high position, he must train his subordinates and trust them. They must relieve him of all small matters. He must be set free to think, to travel, to plan, to see important customers, to make improvements, to do all the big jobs of leadership.*
>
> HERBERT N CASSON

The Criteria For Performance Excellence (CPE)

In your response, answer the following questions:

a. Vision, Values, and Mission

1. **Vision and Values:** How do senior leaders set your organization's vision and values? How do senior leaders deploy the vision and values through your leadership system, to the workforce, to key suppliers and partners, and to customers and other stakeholders, as appropriate? How do senior leaders' actions reflect a commitment to those values?

2. **Promoting Legal and Ethical Behavior:** How do senior leaders' actions demonstrate their commitment to legal and ethical behavior? How do they promote an organizational environment that requires it?

3. **Creating a Successful Organization:** How do senior leaders' actions build an organization which is successful now and in the future? How do they:

    - Create an environment for the achievement of your mission, improvement of organizational performance, performance leadership, and organizational learning, and learning for people in the workforce?

    - Create a workforce culture that delivers a consistently positive customer experience and fosters customer engagement?

    - Create an environment for innovation and intelligent risk taking, achievement of your strategic objectives, and organizational agility?

    - Participate in succession planning and the development of future organizational leaders?

Notes:

1.1. Your organizational performance results should be reported in items 7.1–7.5. Results related to the effectiveness of leadership and the leadership system should be reported in item 7.4.

1.1a(1). Your organization's vision should set the context for the strategic objectives and action plans you describe in items 2.1 and 2.2.

1.1a(3). A successful organization is capable of addressing current business needs and, through agility and strategic management, is capable of preparing successfully for its future business, market, and operating environment. Achieving future success may require leading transformational changes in the organization's structure and culture. Both external and internal factors should be considered. Factors in your organization's sustainability might include workforce capability and capacity, resource availability, technology, knowledge, core competencies, work systems, facilities, and equipment. Success now and in the future might be affected by changes in the marketplace and customer preferences, in the financial markets, and in the legal and regulatory environment. In the context of ongoing success, the concept of innovation and taking intelligent risks includes both technological and organizational innovation to help the organization succeed in the future. A successful organization also ensures a safe and secure environment for its workforce and other key stakeholders. A successful organization is capable of addressing risks and opportunities arising from environmental considerations and climate change.

NIST (2015–2016) pp. 7–8

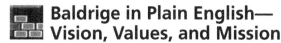 Baldrige in Plain English— Vision, Values, and Mission

This Area to Address initiates an entire organization's focus on performance excellence as an effective business model (such as a focus on the use of the Criteria for Performance Excellence—CPE). If the leaders are not involved in the journey it will not work as a viable business model. They cannot delegate the commitment to the journey and expect anything tangible or valuable to happen down through the organization. Everyone down the organization knows what the boss values—look at his or her calendar to see where he or she spends their time. This Area to Address starts with what the senior leaders (the head of the organization, and that person's direct reports) believe, do, expect, and verify.

Vision and Values

Clearly, senior leaders must define where the organization is headed, what they want the organization to be, the organization's values (and other beliefs), and acceptable behaviors during the journey. Frequently the shortcoming is not the lack of values, as many organizations have beautiful plaques on the wall touting a fairly routine set of values or beliefs. The shortcoming is the inability to translate the beliefs and values into behaviors and practices and then the lack of discipline to practice those behaviors every day in every transaction. This is where the development of a Leadership System is key. It is not intuitive what a "systematic approach to lead" might include, but through a Leadership System, the organization can begin to ensure that every leader, at every level, leads in the manner the senior leaders endorse.

The senior leaders must, at all times, emulate the behaviors they want to see throughout the organization. When senior leaders do that, they must also ensure that leaders at all levels in the organization are themselves role models 100% of the time for these foundational beliefs to be taken seriously. If the leaders do not act as role models all of the time, the behaviors and culture changes they desire in the organization will not take place.

Everyone will clearly understand that what the leader says and what he or she does, or will tolerate, are two different things. As one Baldrige recipient CEO put it, "When I asked why the people were not making the changes necessary to transform the organization, the answer I got back was, 'We'll change when the CEO changes!'" Put more simply, a leader's actions *must* speak so loudly that nobody can hear what they are saying. No leader can get away with the old axiom "Do as I say, not as I do."

Promoting Legal and Ethical Behavior

Once leaders set the organizational beliefs, vision, mission, values, purpose, or other foundational factors, they must communicate them so clearly that all employees understand what the organization stands for, what the organization believes, their role, and how they are expected to act. The organizational environment must foster, require, and measure legal, regulatory, and ethical compliance of each leader and employee.

After the foundational beliefs, leaders must set the direction. This must be for both short- and long-term time horizons. Additionally, the overall direction and each group's or person's responsibilities for moving in the desired direction must be clear for the organization to be effective and sustainable. Ensuring this sustainability is a key job of senior leadership. The direction set must ensure that the organization will remain viable and sustainable both operationally (short-term) and strategically (long-term).

Creating a Successful Organization

Once leaders have established a foundation of beliefs, set the direction of the organization, and clearly established and communicated expectations, it is then their responsibility to create an environment where people can do their best in achieving their objectives. Leaders need to implement specific processes to ensure empowerment, employees understand their level of empowerment, and they have the opportunity to improve, innovate, and learn. These processes must create an environment for organizational, personal and workforce learning, innovation, and competitive and role-model performance. To achieve this, leaders (at every level of the organization) must drive organizational agility. This can only be accomplished if those leaders use defined processes (and the associated decision Criteria within those processes), review performance, and drive actions at short intervals. One area where leaders must be role models is in their assessment and improvement of their personal leadership skills. If leaders do not try to improve themselves, why should anybody else try to improve? These senior leaders must also guide the development of future organizational leaders, and participate in succession planning.

To be a short-term success, an organization must ensure it has:

- People
- Critical skills
- Money
- Data
- Facilities
- Equipment
- An environment of safety
- Supply chain

If one of these is missing, the organization will fail quickly.

To be a long-term success, the leaders must embrace:

- Creation of an environment for the achievement of mission
- Improvement of organizational performance
- Performance leadership
- Organizational learning, and learning for people in the workforce
- Creation of a workforce culture that delivers a consistently positive customer experience and fosters customer engagement
- Creation of an environment for innovation and intelligent risk taking
- Creation of an environment for the achievement of strategic objectives
- Organizational agility
- Participation in (effective) succession planning and the development of future organizational leaders

If one of these is missing, the organization will fail over the longer term.

Summary

All of item 1.1 focuses on how senior leaders establish the culture. It outlines the actions senior leaders must model if they want the other layers of the organization to perform effectively. Leaders must also ensure that these actions are adopted. This is true for all of item 1.1, but is particularly true for Area to Address 1.1a, where the leaders establish a foundation for all other leadership responsibilities.

1.1b COMMUNICATION AND ORGANIZATIONAL PERFORMANCE

> *It is an immutable law in business that words are words, explanations are explanations, promises are promises but only performance is reality.*
>
> HAROLD S. GENEEN

The Criteria For Performance Excellence (CPE)

In your response, include answers to the following questions:

b. Communication and Organizational Performance

1. **Communication:** How do senior leaders communicate with and engage the entire workforce and key customers? How do they:

   - Encourage frank, two-way communication, including effective use of social media when appropriate?
   - Communicate key decisions and needs for organizational change?
   - Reinforce high performance and a customer and business focus by taking a direct role in motivating the workforce, including by participating in reward and recognition programs?

2. **Focus on Action:** How do senior leaders create a focus on action that will achieve the organization's mission? How do senior leaders:

- Create a focus on action that will improve the organization's performance, achieve innovation and intelligent risk taking, and attain its vision?
- Identify needed actions?
- Set expectations for organizational performance, include a focus on creating and balancing value for customers and other stakeholders?

Notes:

1.1b(1). Use of social media may include delivering periodic messages through internal and external web sites, tweets, blogging, and customer and workforce electronic forums, as well as monitoring external web sites and blogs and responding, when appropriate.

1.1b(1). *Nonprofit organizations that rely on volunteers to accomplish their work should also discuss efforts to communicate with and engage the volunteer workforce.*

1.1b(2). Senior leaders' focus on action considers your strategy, workforce, work systems, and assets. It includes taking intelligent risks and implementing innovations and ongoing improvements in productivity that may be achieved by eliminating waste or reducing cycle time; improvement efforts might use techniques such as PDCA, Six Sigma, and Lean. Senior leaders' focus on action also includes the actions needed to achieve your strategic objectives (see 2.2a[1]) and may involve establishing change management plans for major organizational change or responding rapidly to significant information from social media or other input.

NIST (2015–2016) p. 7

Baldrige in Plain English—Communication and Organizational Performance

In Area to Address 1.1a, the leaders established what is important in the organization, the organization's overall direction, and the culture, which is focused on legal and ethical behavior and fostering high performance to ensure sustainability.

This Area to Address, 1.1b, follows these foundations with a description of leaders' roles and responsibilities in institutionalizing the culture. Leaders must provide the organization and employees with the leadership, communication, empowerment, and motivation needed to drive organizational performance down to the action level. As with the earlier Area to Address 1.1a, 1.1b discusses the responsibilities that senior leaders cannot delegate.

Communication

This Area asks how leaders communicate and how they are involved in engaging the workforce. This includes initiating frank two-way communication, communicating the key decisions, ensuring that the appropriate employees understand the key decisions, and taking an active role in the reward and recognition programs in a manner that reinforces high performance, a customer focus, and a business focus. The bottom line of 1.1b is a leader's role in driving the high performance of the organization and of all employees.

Clarity of direction is the foundation for deploying the organization's direction from the top down to every employee. In fact, great leaders often see one of their most important roles as the clear and consistent communication of direction. Once the direction is set, leaders must ensure their performance expectations are clearly communicated throughout the organization to every employee, supplier, partner, owner, stakeholder, and in some cases to the community as a whole. Now, the CPE further asserts that an organization needs to understand the breadth and depth of their communications. Organizations need to understand: 1) which communication methods are two-way, 2) which methods are one-way, and 3) for the two–way communication, by using measures or tangible validation, how leadership ensures that the two-way communication process is effective.

It is implicit in high-performing organizations that leaders create a culture where all information, including bad news, can quickly ascend to the ears of leadership. That does not mean all leaders must take action themselves because the best people may already be working on the problem, but it does mean the organization communicates in an open and transparent manner. Problems are quickly communicated and addressed, and the "fix" to problems involves improving processes, not just blaming individuals.

Focus on Action

Leaders must drive action. To do this, the CPE asks how leaders review performance, how they use these reviews to assess where they are, and how they decide what actions need to be taken on a short- and long-term basis. This organizational performance review itself is addressed in Area to Address 4.1b in the Criteria. Leaders must ensure that the organizational-level objectives are translated to every team at a minimum or, preferably, to every employee. Senior leaders must be able to understand what actions are needed, and ensure that those actions:

- Are linked to the higher-level goals or objectives
- Flow down the organization effectively to actions at the lowest level
- Have sufficient resources allocated to them
- Are tracked and appropriate changes are made based on actual performance (agility)
- Ultimately are achieved

Additionally, during the process to establish the organization's objectives, leaders must understand the needs and expectations of all stakeholders. The goal is to develop generative solutions that create value for multiple stakeholders vs. simply reallocating resources among the stakeholders. Leaders must:

- Understand customer and stakeholder requirements
- Determine which requirements will be met (balance the overall value they will support)
- Plan the balance
- Resource the balance
- Deploy the balance
- Track the achievement of the balance
- Adjust to ensure the achievement of the balance based on actual performance
- Achieve the balance
- Assess the impact of achieving the balance on the customers and other stakeholders

New to the Criteria this year is the term *Intelligent Risk Taking*. A complete definition is included in the Glossary, but simply, this is the ability to ensure that the appropriate analysis has taken place so leaders can manage with data (one of the Baldrige Core Values is Management-By-Fact). Additionally, an increased emphasis is placed on innovation and driving discontinuous change at all levels of the organization.

1.2 Governance and Societal Responsibilities

1.2a ORGANIZATIONAL GOVERNANCE

The best and noblest lives are those which are set toward high ideals.

RENE' ALEMERAS

The Criteria For Performance Excellence (CPE)

In your response, include answers to the following questions:

a. Organizational Governance

1. **Governance System:** How does your organization ensure responsible governance? How does your organization review and achieve the following key aspects of its governance system:
   - Accountability for senior leaders' actions
   - Accountability for strategic plans
   - Fiscal accountability
   - Transparency in operations
   - Selection of governance board members, and disclosure policies for them, as appropriate
   - Independence and effectiveness of internal and external audits
   - Protection of stakeholder and stockholder interests, as appropriate
   - Succession planning for senior leaders

2. **Performance Evaluation:** How do you evaluate the performance of your senior leaders, including the chief executive, and your governance board? How do you use these performance evaluations in determining executive

compensation? How do your senior leaders and governance board use these performance evaluations to advance their development and improve both their own effectiveness as leaders and that of your board and leadership system, as appropriate?

Notes:

1.2. Societal responsibilities in areas critical to your ongoing marketplace success should also be addressed in Strategy Development (item 2.1) and Operations Focus (Category 6). Key results should be reported as Leadership and Governance Results (item 7.4). Examples are results related to regulatory and legal requirements (including the results of mandated financial audits); reductions in environmental impacts through the use of green technology, resource-conserving activities, reduction of carbon footprint, or other means; or improvements in social impacts, such as the global use of enlightened labor practices.

1.2. The health and safety of your workforce are not addressed in this item; you should address these workforce factors in items 5.1 and 6.2.

1.2.a(1). The governance board's review of organizational performance and progress, if appropriate, is addressed in 4.1(b).

1.2a(1). Transparency in the operations of your governance system should include your internal controls on governance processes. For some privately-held businesses and nonprofit organizations, an external advisory board may provide some or all governance board functions. For nonprofit organizations that serve as stewards of public funds, stewardship of those funds and transparency in operations are areas of emphasis.

1.2a(2). The evaluation of leaders' performance might be supported by peer reviews, formal performance manage¬ment reviews, and formal or informal feedback from and surveys of the workforce and other stakeholders. For some privately-held businesses and nonprofit and government organizations, external advisory boards might evaluate the performance of senior leaders and the governance board.

NIST (2015–2016) pp. 8–9

Baldrige in Plain English—Organizational Governance

Governance System

For governance to be effective, it is not enough to have slogans on the wall or policies and procedures that extol the importance of integrity, ethics, values, and governance. The actual behavior that demonstrates these qualities should be implemented down to each and every employee and transaction. Governance has to be "role modeled" by every leader, every day. There are no "time outs" when a leader can act in a manner not befitting a role model.

At one of the most recent *Quest for Excellence* conferences (where the new Baldrige Recipients tell their stories for the first time), one of the Baldrige recipients was asked how companies can ensure that "no employee ever does something wrong." The Baldrige recipient's answer was simple, "We can't!" He went on to explain that leaders must establish a governance structure, metrics, training, systematic processes for governance, and monitoring for compliance, each of which can be consistently evaluated and improved. In the final analysis, however, individuals must execute the daily transactions every day. The system needs to be clear on the appropriate work instructions so employees know how to do their job in an acceptable manner, clear on the rules, clear on both external and internal audits, and clear on the consequences of actions which do not fall within the acceptable guidelines.

Senior leaders must ensure that all employees—and particularly the leaders—are accountable for their actions, that they are accountable for the strategic plans, that there is adequate fiscal accountability, that operations are transparent enough that they can be audited, and that all stakeholder and stockholder interests are effectively protected. To achieve these goals, the CPE asks how the organization ensures independence in external and internal audits. Finally, succession planning for senior leaders must emphasize the values and behaviors endorsed by the organization.

This is impacted by the selection of governance board members and disclosure policies for them. Both internal and external audits must be independent and effective.

While an organization or its leaders cannot eliminate the possibility of someone doing something wrong, they can reduce the likelihood. Governance, like all the other parts of Categories 1 through 6, must be implemented through a systematic process—a process that is defined, measured, stabilized, and improved.

Performance Evaluation

Finally, the Criteria asks how the organization evaluates leadership performance, including the performance and compensation of the chief executive, the governance board, and the oversight board or board of directors. In this manner, the examiners can understand how the board reviews performance and how they evaluate the board and their personal effectiveness. These need to be tangible measures, tracking and audits, with tangible actions taken to follow up on concerns or non-conformances.

These measures, reviews, and results should be used to advance the development of senior leaders, to improve their personal leadership effectiveness, and that of their governance board and leadership board. As with other parts of the business model, these improvements need to be systematic. In addition to the evaluation and improvement of the leadership groups, which are at the top of the organization, performance improvement needs to be inculcated into every leader at every level. This needs to be systematically achieved through the leadership system.

1.2b LEGAL AND ETHICAL BEHAVIOR

In the arena of human life the honors and rewards fall
To those who show their good qualities in action.

ARISTOTLE

The Criteria For Performance Excellence (CPE)

In your response, include answers to the following questions:

b. Legal and Ethical Behavior

1. **Legal and Regulatory Compliance:** How do you anticipate and address public concerns with your products and operations? How do you:
   - Address any adverse impacts of your products and operations?
   - Anticipate public concerns with your current and future products and operations?

- Prepare for these impacts and concerns proactively, including through conservation of natural resources and effective supply-chain management processes, as appropriate?

What are your key compliance processes, measures, and goals for meeting and surpassing regulatory and legal requirements, as appropriate? What are your key processes, measures, and goals for addressing risks associated with your products and operations?

2. **Ethical Behavior:** How do you promote and ensure ethical behavior in all interactions? What are your key processes and measures or indicators for enabling and monitoring ethical behavior in your governance structure, throughout your organization, and in interactions with your workforce, customers, partners, suppliers, and other stakeholders? How do you monitor and respond to breaches of ethical behavior?

Notes:

1.2b(1). Nonprofit organizations should report, as appropriate, how they meet and surpass the regulatory and legal requirements and standards that govern fundraising and lobbying.

1.2b(2). Measures or indicators of ethical behavior might include the percentage of independent board members, measures of relationships with stockholder and non-stockholder constituencies, instances of ethical conduct or compliance breaches and responses to them, survey results showing workforce perceptions of organizational ethics, ethics hotline use, and results of ethics reviews and audits. Measures or indicators of ethical behavior might also include evidence that policies, workforce training, and monitoring systems are in place for conflicts of interest; protection and use of sensitive data, information, and knowledge generated through synthesizing and correlating these data; and proper use of funds are in place.

NIST (2015–2016) pp. 8–9

Baldrige in Plain English—Legal and Ethical Behavior

Governance (item 1.2a) addresses the appropriate transparency and checks and balances. Similarly, legal and ethical behavior needs 100% compliance, and internal and external checks and balances.

Does the organization address public concerns, handle all transactions ethically, and support the key communities where it operates? In addition, does it ensure that all transactions of the organization meet the appropriate legal and ethical standards?

Legal and Regulatory Compliance

The first part of Area to Address 1.2b assesses whether or not the organization understands the "footprint" it leaves on the world it operates within. This section includes an organization's understanding of its impact on the public and society from:

- The *products* the organization produces
- The *services* the organization renders and provides
- The organization's internal *operations*, including the processes and materials used

In recent years, the Criteria for Performance Excellence (CPE) has turned its focus from merely meeting regulatory and legal requirements to anticipating and surpassing regulatory and legal requirements. This shift is most likely based on the belief that the regulatory and legal requirements will not diminish over time, but, quite possibly, will continue to become more stringent.

The CPE model challenges organizations to identify the key compliance processes, to determine how these processes are measured, and how goals have been set. It recognizes how the organization understands these processes, measures, and goals, and how it uses them to assess risk. Risks also need to be assessed for the organization's key products, services, and operations.

Moving from the current products, services, and operations to the future, CPE wants an organization to understand the process used to anticipate what could happen. The specific question starts with "How do you anticipate public concerns?" The CPE model identifies how the organization anticipates concerns and what the organization is doing to prepare for those concerns if they should occur. Being proactive is more favorable than being behind the regulatory power curve and trying to catch up once public concerns drive new regulations.

Ethical Behavior

The CPE also focuses on establishing an ethical foundation throughout the organization. This starts with understanding the organizational culture [requested in the Organizational Profile, [(P.1a(2)]. It is further discussed in Area to Address 1.1a(1), which asks how leaders set and deploy organizational values.

The CPE aims to ensure that ethical behavior is deployed throughout the entire organization at all times. As with other "how" questions, this area looks for a specific systematic process. The CPE want to know how the processes are used, how well they are deployed, and how they are measured. Interestingly, the CPE does not ask for specific goals for ethical behavior. It may be assumed that any company would have a goal of no ethical violations. Nevertheless, actual ethical performance can be reported in item 7.4 in the Results Category.

Ethical behavior is to be monitored throughout the organization. It is also to be monitored with key partners, including suppliers, customers, community, and others. In simple terms, the CPE wants to ensure that ethical behavior is everywhere all the time. Although this compliance is difficult for any company to guarantee, the CPE model looks for processes, measures, and checks and balances to ensure that processes have been effectively implemented and are effectively enforced.

1.2c SOCIETAL RESPONSIBILITIES

> *To give away money is an easy matter, and in any man's power. But to decide to whom to give it, and how large and when, and for what purpose and how, is neither in every man's power – nor an easy matter. Hence it is that such excellence is rare, praiseworthy, and noble.*
>
> ARISTOTLE

The Criteria For Performance Excellence (CPE)

In your response, include answers to the following questions:

c. Societal Responsibilities

1. **Societal Well-Being:** How do you consider societal well-being and benefit as part of your strategy and daily operations? How do you contribute to the well-being of your environmental, social, and economic systems?

2. **Community Support:** How do you actively support and strengthen your key communities? What are your key communities? How do you identify them and determine areas for organizational involvement, including areas that leverage your core competencies? How do your senior leaders, in concert with your workforce, contribute to improving these communities?

Notes:

1.2c. Areas of societal contributions and community sup¬port might include your efforts to improve the environment (for example, collaboration to conserve the environment or natural resources); strengthen local community services, education, health, and emergency preparedness; and improve the practices of trade, business, or professional associations.

1.2c. *Some charitable organizations may contribute to society and support their key communities totally through mission-related activities. In such cases, it is appropriate to respond with any "extra efforts" through which you support these communities.*

NIST (2015–2016) p. 9

Baldrige in Plain English— Societal Responsibilities

The CPE has evolved to include an increased emphasis on the three key dimensions of success now and in the future—economic, environmental, and societal, or as Elkington, Emerson, and Beloe (2006) call it—the "triple bottom line." Including these in the Leadership Category allows these concepts to permeate the organization's systems including strategy, operations, scorecard, and so forth.

Organizations of all types are facing increasing pressures from a variety of stakeholders, including customers, employees, investors, and the public to operate in ways that not only make money but also are good for the environment and society as a whole (Grant, 2007 and Latham, 2008). Many customers are making purchase decisions based on the environmental performance of the products and services, and on the environmental record of the company. Employees want to work for organizations that are "good citizens" and have a good environmental and societal record. Many investors now recognize the risks involved with companies that have poor environmental practices. For example, the profitability could change quickly for companies with a high carbon "footprint" if the government puts a price on carbon either through a carbon tax or a cap and trade system. To help investors assess the risk of companies, the Carbon Disclosure Project provides reports that describe the risks for each company, how well they are doing in addressing those risks, and their plans to improve. In addition, organizations are facing increasing pressures from a variety of influential organizations representing various stakeholder groups including the Intergovernmental Panel on Climate Change (IPCC) and the United Nations Framework Convention on Climate Change (UNFCCC). What seems clear is the bar is being raised once again and organizations are challenged with figuring out how to create value for multiple stakeholders.

Some have proposed that organizations simply cannot afford to do business in an environmentally sound way and still make money. This was the same argument that many proposed when U.S. companies were faced with competitors who were producing higher quality products and services and taking market share. Organizations eventually discovered that high quality resulted in reduced cost and increased market share. Many organizations that score high on the CPE maturity model have become quite good at "connecting the dots." This same thinking used to improve the organization "system" to create value for employees, customers, and investors can be used to add additional stakeholders and requirements into the enterprise model and avoid the zero-sum game of reallocating resources from one stakeholder to another.

In support of key communities, many organizations list all of the activities that they participate in and support. As impressive as these laundry lists may be, they miss the point of the CPE. The CPE is looking for a process and decision criteria within it, used by the organization to address societal needs.

Societal Well-Being

When the CPE asks how the organization supports key communities, it is looking for a systematic set of steps that the organization follows to be proactive in their community support. This includes how the organization considers societal well-being and benefit as a part of the strategy, as well as how it is considered on a daily basis and as a part of daily operations. The CPE also emphasizes how the organization considers the environmental, social, and economic benefit of this support. Many organizations, however, simply prioritize the vast list of requests they receive from their community for ongoing support. The CPE, in seeking a process, is asking companies to be more proactive and less reactive in aligning the community support with their organizational beliefs, needs, and interests.

Community Support

To establish the foundation for support of key communities, the Criteria seeks to understand how key communities are determined and how emphasis for organizational involvement is decided. Both of those questions require clear processes and decision criteria.

Most organizations identify key communities as the predominant communities in which they do business and in which their employees live. As simple as these decision criteria are, they do meet the criterion of being clear enough to support a process. Beyond deciding what the organization's key communities are, the Criteria asks for the organization to list them, and then discusses how the organization decides to become involved. Simple logic for community support would include questions such as the following:

- How does the organization decide what it wants to support?
- How does the organization decide whether or not a specific activity qualifies or is a match with what it wants to support?
- How does the organization listen to what is going on in the community in order to be proactive in implementing the use of their decision criteria?
- How does the organization decide whether or not a specific activity warrants senior executive involvement?

Once the overall systematic process is described, the laundry list of community activities no longer consists of an anecdotal examples, but rather examples of deployment of the systematic approach. It can also show how the organization has used the process and decision Criteria to support the community. Area 1.2c is a key area where an organization needs to demonstrate a systematic process. Many organizations do not answer using processes, but only use examples of community support activities.

Category 2—Strategy

2.1 Strategy Development

2.1a STRATEGY DEVELOPMENT PROCESS

Wake Up! You are not just a bunch of departments! The output of the Strategic Planning Process should be effective integration of the external challenges with the internal capabilities. This should result in aligning both process capabilities and detailed actions to take you to the future.

WALT MATWIJEC

The Criteria For Performance Excellence (CPE)

> In your response, include answers to the following questions:
>
> a. Strategy Development Process
>
> 1. **Strategic Planning Process:** How do you conduct your strategic planning? What are the key process steps? Who are the key participants? What are your short- and longer-term planning horizons? How are they addressed in the planning process? How does your strategic planning process address the potential need for
>
>   - Transformational change and prioritization of change initiatives?
>   - Organizational agility?
>   - Operational flexibility?

2. **Innovation:** How does your strategy development process stimulate and incorporate innovation? How do you identify strategic opportunities? How do you decide which strategic opportunities are intelligent risks for pursuing? What are your key strategic opportunities?

3. **Strategy Considerations:** How do you collect and analyze relevant data and develop information for your strategic planning process? In this collection and analysis, how do you include these key elements:

    - Your strategic challenges and strategic advantages
    - Risks to your organization's future success
    - Potential blind spots in your strategic planning process and information
    - Your ability to execute the strategic plan

4. **Work Systems and Core Competencies:** What are your key work systems? How do you make work system decisions that facilitate the accomplishment of your strategic objectives? How do you decide which key processes will be accomplished by external suppliers and partners? How do those decisions consider your core competencies and the core competencies of potential suppliers and partners? How do you determine future organizational core competencies and work systems?

Notes:

2.1. This item deals with your overall organizational strategy, which might include changes in product offerings and customer engagement processes. However, you should describe the product design and customer engagement strategies, respectively, in items 6.1 and 3.2, as appropriate.

2.1. *Strategy development* refers to your organization's approach to preparing for the future. In developing your strategy, you might use various types of forecasts, projec¬tions, options, scenarios, knowledge (see 4.2a for relevant organizational knowledge), analyses, or other approaches to envisioning the future in order to make decisions and allocate resources. Strategy development might involve key suppliers, distributors, partners, and customers. For some nonprofit organizations, strategy development might involve organizations providing similar services or drawing from the same donor population or volunteer workforce.

2.1. The term *strategy* should be interpreted broadly. Strategy might be built around or lead to any or all of the following: new products; redefinition of key customer groups or market segments; differentiation of your brand; new core competencies; revenue growth via various approaches, including acquisitions, grants, and endowments; divestitures; new partnerships and alliances; and new employee or volunteer relationships. Strategy might be directed toward becoming a preferred supplier, a local supplier in each of your major customers' or partners' markets, low-cost producer, market innovator, or a provider of a high-end or customized product or service. It might also be directed toward meeting a community or public need.

2.1a(2). Strategic opportunities arise from outside-the-box thinking, brainstorming, capitalizing on serendipity, research, and innovation processes; nonlinear extrapolation of current conditions; and other approaches to imagining a different future. The generation of ideas that leads to strategic opportunities benefits from an environment that encourages non-directed, free thought. Choosing which stra¬tegic opportunities to pursue involves considering relative risk, financial and otherwise, and then making intelligent choices or taking intelligent risks.

2.1a(3). Data and information may come from a variety of internal and external sources and in a variety of forms. Data are available in increasingly greater volumes and at greater speeds. The ability to capitalize on data and information, including large datasets (*big data*), is based on the ability to analyze the data, draw conclusions, and pursue actions, including intelligent risks.

2.1a(3). Data and information might relate to customer and market requirements, expectations, and opportunities; your core competencies; the competitive environment and your performance now and in the future relative to competitors and comparable organizations; your product life cycle; technological and other key innovations or changes that might affect your products and services and the way you operate, as well as the rate of innovation; workforce and other resource needs; your ability to capitalize on diversity; opportunities to redirect resources to higher-priority products, services, or areas; financial, societal, ethical, regulatory, technological, security, and other potential risks and opportunities; your ability to prevent and respond to emergencies, including natural or other disasters; changes in the local, national, or global economy; requirements for and strengths and weaknesses of your partners and supply chain; changes in your parent organization; and other factors unique to your organization.

2.1a(3). Your strategic planning should address your ability to mobilize the necessary resources and knowledge to execute the strategic plan. It should also address your ability to execute contingency plans or, if circumstances require, a shift in plans and rapid execution of new or changed plans.

2.1a(4). Decisions about work systems are strategic. These decisions involve protecting intellectual property, capitalizing on core competencies, and mitigating risk. Decisions about your work systems affect organizational design and structure, size, locations, profitability, and ongoing success. In a generic view of an organization, for example, the organization might define three work systems: one that addresses production of the product or service, one that engages the customer, and one that comprises systems that support production and customer engagement.

NIST (2015–2016) pp. 10–11

Baldrige in Plain English— Strategy Development Process

In 2.1 the organization establishes the strategy and begins to translate the direction set by the leaders in item 1.1 into more specific goals and objectives. It is one of the few places in the Criteria for Performance Excellence (CPE) framework where a checklist of issues that need to be addressed is provided.

Strategic Planning Process

The Criteria starts by asking about the overall strategic planning process. Although all of these are not called for in the Criteria, an organization's planning process should include a description of:

- The steps in the planning process
- Who is involved in these steps
- What is *not* asked in the Criteria, but details which will help you to explain you process:
  - What happens in each step
  - The inputs for each step
  - The outputs for each step
  - The documents used or generated in each step
  - The reviews or decisions in each step
  - The decision criteria used for the decisions made

The short- and longer-term time horizons should be clearly defined, including the rationale for choosing them. For example, the time horizons can be chosen to correspond to the organization's planning cycles, customer planning cycles, or other logical (for example, market-based) planning cycles. Market-based reasons for choosing a planning cycle could include industry business cycles, technology cycles, or the time required to increase organizational capacity or capability. In addition, these should establish how the organization is meeting the internal or external strategic needs in the way they have established their planning horizons.

Understanding how the organization determines the need for transformational changes (defined in the Glossary at the back of this book), organizational agility, and operational flexibility is new this year.

Innovation

Throughout the previous 2013–2014 Criteria there was an increased emphasis on innovation. It is mentioned in leadership, planning, and several other points (a count of innovation in the Criteria shows it being mentioned approximately a dozen times). This emphasis has continued into the 2015–2016 Criteria. Innovation is discontinuous improvement, and the implication of the Criteria changes are clear—innovation is the responsibility of everyone, while being led/role modeled by the senior leadership. In item 2.1, the Criteria asks how leaders create an environment that supports innovation, and how they track strategic opportunities, and what are the strategic opportunities. Driving the decisions being made is the analysis being performed to ensure that the decisions are intelligent (intelligent risks). The Criteria asks how the organization decides which strategic opportunities are intelligent risks for pursuing.

Strategy Considerations

When addressing each of the factors to be considered during the planning process, the organization should do so in a manner clear enough for someone reading the assessment document to understand. For example, it is not sufficient to discuss customer and market needs in general terms; there should be a specific point where these are addressed in the planning process in a very clear manner.

The basic belief surrounding the planning process is that several factors need to be assessed during planning. If one of these key factors is not effectively assessed (and the impact of the factor on the plan is not assessed during planning), the implementation of the plan might be hindered by the inability of the organization to understand and respond to one of the factors they should have assessed during planning.

These factors include:

- Your strategic challenges and strategic advantages
- Risks to your organization's future success
- Potential changes in your regulatory environment
- Potential blind spots in your strategic planning process and information
- Your ability to execute the strategic plan

One future success example within these strategy considerations could be if the organization assumes the workforce can support the new plan. If leaders do not formally assess workforce capability and capacity, however, they may not realize that training and development for the new skills are required and that this cannot be accomplished by the time the skills are needed. In this example, the development of those skills may not be a part of the overall plan, or may not be timely, and the plan implementation may fail.

Work Systems and Core Competencies

Determining your Key Work Systems is a strategic decision, and the Criteria now wants to know what are the key work systems, and how you make key decisions, including:

- How do you make key work system decisions that facilitate the accomplishment of your strategic objectives?
- How do you decide which key processes will be accomplished by key suppliers and partners?
- How do your decisions consider your core competency (ies) and the core competency (ies) of potential suppliers and partners?
- How do you determine future core competencies?

Although identifying the key work processes and how they support the key work systems are not specifically asked for in the new Criteria, any organization assessing itself should clearly make such identifications.

2.1b STRATEGIC OBJECTIVES

> *If you can't describe your strategy in twenty minutes, simply and in plain language, you haven't got a plan. 'But,' people may say, 'I've got a complex strategy. It can't be reduced to a page.' That's nonsense. That's not a complex strategy. It's a complex thought about the strategy.*
>
> LARRY BOSSIDY

The Criteria For Performance Excellence (CPE)

In your response, include answers to the following questions:

b. Strategic Objectives

1. **Key Strategic Objectives:** What are your organization's key strategic objectives and timetable for achieving them? What are your most important goals for these strategic objectives? What key changes, if any, are planned in your products, customers and markets, suppliers and partners, and operations?

2. **Strategic Objective Considerations:** How do your strategic objectives achieve appropriate balance among varying and potentially competing organization needs? How do your strategic objectives:

- Address your strategic challenges and leverage your core competencies, strategic advantages, and strategic opportunities?
- Balance short- and longer-term time horizons?
- Consider and balance the needs of all key stakeholders?

Notes:

2.1b(1). Strategic objectives might address rapid response, customization, co-location with major customers or partners, workforce capability and capacity, specific joint ventures, virtual manufacturing, rapid or market-changing innovation, ISO quality or environmental systems registration, societal responsibility actions or leadership, social media and web-based supplier and customer relationship management, and product and service quality enhancements. Responses should focus on your specific challenges, advantages, and opportunities—those most important to your ongoing success and to strengthening your overall performance.

NIST (2015–2016) pp, 10–11

Baldrige in Plain English— Strategic Objectives

This area is straightforward. It asks for strategic objectives and when those strategic objectives will be accomplished. It is the output of Area to Address 2.1a.

Key Strategic Objectives

Under the strategic objectives, the CPE asks for the goals the organization hopes to achieve for the strategic objectives and the timeframe for achieving them.

Strategic Challenges and Advantages (P.2b)	Strategic Objectives (2.1b[1])	Long-Term Action Plans (2.2a[1])	Short-Term Action Plans (2.2a[1])
- Business - Operational - Human Resource	- Goals (2.1b(1)) - Measures (not required)	- Projected competitor performance (2.2b) - Timeframe (2.2b) - Organization performance versus competitor (2.2b) - Timetable (specific dates not required) - Changes in products and services (2.2a(3)) - Measures or indicators (2.2a(5)) - Goals (not required) - Projections (in timeframe (2.2b))	- Projected competitor performance (2.2b) - Timeframe (2.2b) - Organization performance versus competitor (2.2b) - Timetable (specific dates not required) - Changes in products and services (2.2a(3)) - Measures or indicators (2.2a(5)) - Goals (not required) - Projections (in timeframe (2.2b))

Additionally, the CPE asks the organization to link the strategic objectives back to the strategic challenges identified in P.2b in the Organizational Profile. The overall logic flow suggests that strategic challenges (external) should drive strategic objectives (internal), which should drive strategic goals.

The logic flow from the Organizational Profile to item 2.1 to item 2.2 is as follows:

⇨ **Strategic Challenges:** Understanding what is coming at us from the outside that we must address, but do not control

⇨ **Success Factors:** Understanding what anybody in our business needs to excel at if they wish to remain competitive today. (This was eliminated by Baldrige, but the author still feels it is valuable.)

> ⇨ **Strategic Advantages:** Understanding our organization's strengths vs. the competitors
>
> ⇨ **Strategic Opportunities:** Understanding what is happening in the marketplace (or internally), which is an opportunity the organization can leverage
>
> ⇨ **Strategic Objectives:** Understanding in what areas we will be stronger once our objectives are achieved

Organizations who clearly understand these linkages have an advantage in developing plans that will keep them competitive.

Additionally, the Criteria focuses on how the organization addresses the opportunities for innovation in products, operations, and the business model. This includes understanding how the organization capitalizes on the current core competencies and addresses the potential need for new core competencies.

The CPE asks several questions which relate to balancing the strategic objectives, the deployment of those objectives, short- and long-term timeframes, and balancing the needs of all stakeholders. Typically, organizations do not clearly address these issues. The most appropriate response is to describe how you ensure that the strategic objectives balance these factors using a systematic process. The systematic process used could include specific activities during particular timeframes or planning activities, as well as clear decision criteria for how the organization decides something and when it decides.

> Note: "balancing" does not mean equal attention, equal resources, or equal results. Balancing means that the balance the organization (and the leaders) *intended* is the balance *planned* is the balance *resourced* is the balance *achieved*. For different organizations, the balance could be significantly different. For example, one organization could be a "cash cow" and the balance of the stakeholder focus would be to give the owners a very high return. Another organization could be in a growth phase and the emphasis could be on building capacity and capability.

Finally, the Criteria asks how the organization addresses the ability to adapt to sudden shifts in market conditions. This is similar to numerous other places where the Criteria assess the organizational ability to adjust actions when results or conditions change.

2.2 Strategy Implementation

2.2a ACTION PLAN DEVELOPMENT AND DEPLOYMENT

The essence of strategy is choosing what not to do.

MICHAEL PORTER

The Criteria For Performance Excellence (CPE)

> In your response, include answers to the following questions:
>
> a. Action Plan Development and Deployment
>
> 1. **Action Plans:** What are your key short- and longer-term action plans? What is their relationship to your strategic objectives? How do you develop your action plans?
>
> 2. **Action Plan Implementation:** How do you deploy your action plans? How do you deploy your action plans to your workforce and to key suppliers and partners, as appropriate, to ensure that you achieve your key strategic objectives? How do you ensure that you can sustain the key outcomes of your action plans?
>
> 3. **Resource Allocation:** How do you ensure that financial and other resources are available to support the achieve¬ment of your action plans while you meet current obligations? How do you allocate these resources to support the plans? How do you manage the risks associated with the plans to ensure your financial viability?
>
> 4. **Workforce Plans:** What are your key workforce plans to support your short- and longer-term strategic objectives and action plans? How do the plans address potential impacts on your workforce members and any potential changes in workforce capability and capacity needs?

5. **Performance Measures:** What key performance measures or indicators do you use to track the achievement and effectiveness of your action plans? How does your overall action plan measurement system reinforce organizational alignment?

6. **Performance Projections:** For these key performance measures or indicators, what are your performance projections for your short- and longer-term planning horizons? How does your projected performance on these measures or indicators compare with your projections of the performance of your competitors or comparable organizations and with key benchmarks, as appropriate? If there are gaps in performance against your competitors or comparable organizations, how do you address them?

Notes:

2.2. The development and deployment of your strategy and action plans are closely linked to other Criteria Items. The following are examples of key linkages:

- Item 1.1: How your senior leaders set and communi¬cate organizational direction

- Category 3: How you gather customer and market knowledge as input to your strategy and action plans and to use in deploying action plans

- Category 4: How you measure and analyze data and manage knowledge to support key information needs, support the development of strategy, provide an effective basis for performance measurements, and track progress on achieving strategic objectives and action plans

- Category 5: How you meet workforce capability and capacity needs, determine needs and design your workforce development and learning system, and implement workforce-related changes resulting from action plans

- Category 6: How you address changes to your work processes resulting from action plans

- Item 7.1: specific accomplishments relative to your organizational strategy and action plans

> **2.2a(2).** Action plan implementation and deployment may require modifications in organizational structures and operating modes. Action plan success benefits from visible short-term wins as well as long-term actions.
>
> **2.2a(6).** Measures and indicators of projected performance might include consideration of changes resulting from new ventures; organizational acquisitions or mergers; new value creation; market entry and shifts; new legislative mandates, legal requirements, or industry stands; and significant anticipated innovations in services and technology.
>
> NIST (2015–2016) p. 12

Baldrige in Plain English—Action Plan Development and Deployment

Item 2.1 developed the strategic plan. Item 2.2 asks, "What do you do with the strategic plan?" Clearly it's harder to deploy a plan than to develop a plan.

Action Plans

Specifically, the CPE asks "how" the organization develops action plans to achieve its strategic objectives. This typically involves the organization describing how it takes the highest level strategy and deploys it through each organizational level down to individual goals, or, at a minimum, team goals. Later the Criteria will ask how you make changes in the action plans.

Action Plan Implementation

The ability to directly link the top strategies (plans) down to actions has been described by Baldrige recipients as the most important thing they have accomplished. In recent years, several Baldrige recipients were asked if they could go through the journey again, what they would do differently. A predominance of these winners indicated they would align the organization (top to bottom as discussed in item 2.2) more quickly. "That is where the power is—to have everyone on the same page."

Resource Allocation

Any organization must effectively allocate resources if plans are to be realized. Although the CPE specifically mentions financial resources, the other resources that should be considered include data, people, critical skills, facilities, equipment, a safety environment, supply chain, and many others. This allocation should be in concert with the risk analysis performed by the organization to ensure that the risks associated with the plans are mitigated to ensure organizational sustainability.

After the Criteria addresses the deployment of the strategic objectives down to the action level, as well as the development of the action plans, it seeks to understand how the organization ensures the changes that result from these action plans can be sustained over the longer-term. Once again, a description of a process, rather than detailed activities and best intentions, is necessary.

Workforce Plans

In addition, this Area to Address seeks to understand how the key human resource plans support the overall strategy of the organization. While many organizations are reluctant to develop a human resource plan, it does not have to be overly complex. It should be a plan that considers factors such as skills needed, turnover, development of skills, development of managerial and leadership skills, development of ethics and social value skills, and others. The human resource plan should describe how those skills are going to be trained and developed into the organization. These plans should be compatible with both the short- and longer-term strategic objectives and actions plans. Without the ability to develop people during the course of the year, the organization may be limited in its ability to achieve its strategic plan.

Performance Measures

All plans, goals, and objectives should have measures or indicators for tracking the achievement and effectiveness of their plans. These measures should reinforce the alignment (up and down the organization). Additionally, they should address all key areas where the plans should be deployed.

Performance Projections

This is the only place in the CPE where an organization can get credit for something it has not yet achieved. It asks for projections of performance that will be derived from the action plans, which are driven by the strategy (Note: these linkages should be clear and should start in the Organizational Profile with the external Strategic Challenges). Additionally, the CPE asks how the organization will know how its performance will compare to its competitors' during those same timeframes. This Area to Address requires the organization to project its own performance, project the performance of competitors, and assess the comparison between the two at some point in the future, presumably at least at the end of each planning time frame. Additionally, the basis for these projections needs to be described in enough detail that the projections are clearly plausible. This means the typical "hockey stick" projections that say we are going to be the same in the near future, but "soon" things will get dramatically better. This is only possible if there are plans being implemented that can make things better.

Typically, organizations cannot provide direct competitive comparisons on a pure apples-to-apples basis. These comparisons, therefore, may have to come from industry knowledge or from common data points, which are infrequently gathered. It is important in 2.2b, however, to describe the process used to develop the projections and the assumptions that have been made in determining the organization's and the competitor's projections.

2.2b ACTION PLAN MODIFICATION

When you arrive at your future, will you blame your past?

ROBERT HALF

The Criteria For Performance Excellence (CPE)

> In your response, include answers to the following questions:
>
> b. Action Plan Modification
>
> > How do you establish and implement modified action plans if circumstances require a shift in plans and rapid execution of new plans?
>
> **Notes:**
>
> > **2.2b.** Organizational agility requires the ability to adapt to changing circumstances, both internal and external.
>
> NIST (2015–2016) p. 12

Baldrige in Plain English—Action Plan Modification

Action Plan Modification

Finally, this Area to Address asks how the organization aligns the overall action plans up to the strategic plan and how they are modified if circumstances require as shift in plans and rapid execution of new plans. Simply stated, the Criteria for Performance Excellence (CPE) asks the organization to check the validity of the action plans and their ability to drive the achievement of the higher level organizational strategy, even if circumstances change.

In changing these action plans, everyone impacted must be systematically included. This means suppliers, partners, collaborators, and others whose actions impact the organization's ability to meet its strategic objectives and action plans.

Category 3—Customer

3.1 *Voice of the Customer*

3.1a CUSTOMER LISTENING

You can't just ask customers what they want and then try to give that to them. By the time you get it built, they'll want something new.

STEVE JOBS

The Criteria For Performance Excellence (CPE)

> In your response, include answers to the following questions:
>
> a. Customer Listening
>
> 1. **Current Customers:** How do you listen to, interact with, and observe customers to obtain actionable information? How do your listening methods vary for different customers, customer groups, or market segments? How do you use social media and web-based technologies to listen to customers, as appropriate? How do your listening methods vary across the customer life cycle? How do you seek immediate and actionable feedback from customers on the quality of products, customer support, and transactions?

2. **Potential Customers:** How do you listen potential customers to obtain actionable information? How do you listen to former customers, potential customers, and competitors' customers to obtain actionable information on your products, customer support, and transactions, as appropriate?

Notes:

3.1. The *voice of the customer* refers to your process for capturing customer-related information. Voice-of-the-customer processes are intended to be proactive and continuously innovative so that they capture stated, unstated, and anticipated customer requirements, expectations, and desires. The goal is customer engagement. In listening to the voice of the customer, you might gather and integrate various types of customer data, such as survey data, focus group findings, blog comments and data from other social media, warranty data, marketing and sales information, and complaint data that affect customers' purchasing and engagement decisions.

3.1. For additional considerations on the products and business of nonprofit organizations, see the notes to P.1a(1) and P.2b.

3.1a(1). Social media and web-based technologies are a growing mode of gaining insight into how customers perceive all aspects of your involvement with them. Listening through social media may include monitoring comments on social media outlets you moderate, as well as on those you do not control such as wikis, online forums, and blogs other than your own.

3.1a(1). The customer life cycle begins in the product concept or pre-sale period and continues through all stages of your involvement with the customer. These stages might include relationship building, the active business relationship, and an exit strategy, as appropriate.

NIST (2015–2016) p. 13

Baldrige in Plain English—Customer Listening

This Area to Address focuses on how the organization listens to customers to understand their needs, wants, and desires to form the development and improvement of products and services.

Listening to Current Customers

In the Organizational Profile, the CPE asks who the customer groups are, and what their requirements are. These customer requirements should be segmented by customer group, in other words, how we group our customers should be based on their requirements; target customer segments, in other words how we sell to them; or market segments, in other words, how the industry or marketplace groups customers or product offerings. Area to Address 3.2a asks how the organization systematically through the process and Criteria determines the customer segments.

Within each of these segments, it is important to have an appropriate range of both formal and informal listening posts. These need to be current enough to give the organization an understanding of what can cause marketplace damage in time to fix the problem before the damage actually occurs. In the 2011–2012 Criteria, the concept of use of social media and web-based technologies was introduced to help to ensure that the information was easy for the customer to provide, and thus is timely. Throughout the 2015–2016 Criteria, the use of social media has been strengthened.

These listening posts may vary for each of the customer groups, and across each stage of the customer life cycle, as a customer (or potential customer) moves through the following life cycle chain:

- Not knowing about the organization
- Knowing about the organization
- Trying the organization
- Liking the organization
- Being loyal to the organization
- Being an advocate for the organization

Once this listening is gathered, the key is how quickly and effectively the appropriate actions are formulated, taken, verified, and improved.

Listening to Potential Customers

This same cycle of listening, planning, and action needs to be taken for former customers, potential customers, and customers of competitors. In all cases, the key is actionable information and the ability to measure the effectiveness of the actions taken.

Once the organization describes how information is gathered from the listening and learning techniques (Area to Address 3.1a), the question becomes "How is the information analyzed to determine, modify, or anticipate changes in customer needs for those product offerings?" This includes analysis of data from current customers, potential customers, future customers, and customers of competitors.

As with other Areas to Address in Category 3, the organization should consider the customer needs during the life cycle of the customer. Although not stated, it is logical to assume that the organization also needs to understand the customer's needs during the product and service life cycles as well. This is particularly true for durable products. For example, our local coffee shop would not need to survey the customers to understand the customers' needs at the beginning, middle, and end of drinking a cup of coffee. An automotive manufacturer, however, needs to understand the customer's needs (and maintenance and support requirements) during the various phases of a car's life.

From this analysis, how does the organization become more customer-focused? (Some organizations use the term *customer-centric*.) Simply stated, if the organization truly understands what drives customers' purchase behaviors, it can compete more effectively in the marketplace than if it does not have that understanding.

3.1b   DETERMINATION OF CUSTOMER SATISFACTION AND ENGAGEMENT

> *There is only one boss. The customer. And he can fire everybody in the company from the chairman on down, simply by spending his money somewhere else.*
>
> SAM WALTON

The Criteria For Performance Excellence (CPE)

In your response, include answers to the following questions:

b. Determination of Customer Satisfaction and Engagement

1. **Satisfaction, Dissatisfaction, and Engagement:** How do you determine customer satisfaction, dissatisfaction, and engagement? How do your determination methods differ among your customer groups and market segments, as appropriate? How do your measurements capture actionable information to use in exceeding your customers' expectations and securing your customers' engagement for the long term?

2. **Satisfaction Relative to Competitors:** How do you obtain information on your customers' satisfaction with your organization relative to other organizations? How do you obtain information on your customers' satisfaction:

   - Relative to their satisfaction with your competitors?

   - Relative to the satisfaction of customers of other organizations that provide similar products or to industry benchmarks, as appropriate?

Notes:

3.1b. You might use any or all of the following to determine customer satisfaction and dissatisfaction: surveys, formal and informal feedback, customer account histories, complaints, field reports, win/loss analysis, customer referral rates, and transaction completion rates. You might gather information on the web, through personal contact or a third party, or by mail. Determining customer dissatisfaction should be seen as being more than reviewing low customer satisfaction scores. Dissatisfaction should be independently determined to identify root causes and enable a systematic remedy to avoid future dissatisfaction.

> **3.1b(2).** Information you obtain on relative customer satisfaction may involve comparisons with competitors, comparisons with other organizations that deliver similar products in a non-competitive marketplace, or comparisons obtained through trade or other organizations. Information obtained on relative customer satisfaction may also involve determining why customers chose your competitors over you.
>
> NIST (2015–2016) pp. 13–14

Baldrige in Plain English—Determination of Customer Satisfaction and Engagement

Once the organization has developed its overall relationship with the customer, segmented the customers, and determined their needs and expectations, the CPE asks how the organization knows whether customers are satisfied, loyal, and engaged. This means asking if the organization's customers value what the organization does enough to come back over and over, help the organization get better, and be an advocate for the organization and their products and services.

There is an understanding in the CPE community that satisfied customers may or may not return to buy products and services. Loyal customers, however, do return to repurchase products and services; hence the term *loyalty*. Finally, engaged customers have an investment in or commitment to the organization's brand and product and service offerings, and are willing to take their time to help.

In the final analysis, the CPE tries to understand whether the organization can correlate its actions (through the organization's processes) to what the customer values, what the customer will pay for, and ultimately to the customers' behavior.

Satisfaction, Dissatisfaction, and Engagement

The CPE asks how the organization determines its customers' satisfaction, engagement (loyalty), and dissatisfaction. These determination methods can and often should vary for different customers and different customer groups. Organizations segment customers because they have different needs and requirements. The CPE asks how an organization knows if it is exceeding customer requirements (customer results data in item 7.1)—another way to drive customer loyalty—and if they are able to "secure their future business" (customer engagement (loyalty) reported in Area to Address 7.2a[2]).

The CPE asks for a description of the organization's relationship with the customer after providing products, services, or transactions (Area to Address 3.2). The classic example of this type of relationship is one where an employee contacts the customer by phone after the product or service is delivered in order to understand the customer's satisfaction with the overall transaction as well as their initial satisfaction with the product or service. Today, social media is helping organizations accomplish this task.

Satisfaction Relative to Competitors

The CPE stretches the organization by asking how it obtains or uses information about its customer satisfaction relative to the customer satisfaction of competitors or industry benchmarks. In some industries, this knowledge is difficult, if not impossible to gather. For example, in some governmental customer relationships (supplying to public sector customers), it is illegal to obtain and to have this information. In this instance, there is no expectation that the organization would attempt to gather the information.

The CPE does not expect an organization to perform any action that is not 100% honest and ethical. Nevertheless, some organizations have not considered benchmarking sources that can help them compare their performance to other high performing groups. For example, organizations can ask customers how the organization ranks with their other suppliers. Even if the customers will not disclose which of their suppliers perform at which levels, they may still reveal where they rank in the pack.

Finally, in the past the CPE asked how the organization kept the survey methods, contact methods, or customer satisfactions and dissatisfaction methods current. Although not as clearly stated in the current Criteria, this is still a valid question. How do you know when the customer is tired of your surveys and how do you respond by updating your customer satisfaction processes?

Dissatisfaction

This needs to be done early enough to capture actionable information, which can prevent the loss of a customer. The actions taken should improve the organization's ability to meet or exceed the customer's current and future requirements.

It should be noted that low customer satisfaction is not the same as dissatisfaction. Dissatisfaction is an overt condition where the customer complains, or asks the organization to take action to correct a condition the customer does not feel should continue.

3.2 Customer Engagement

3.2a PRODUCT OFFERINGS AND CUSTOMER SUPPORT

The purpose of a business is to create a customer.

PETER DRUCKER

 The Criteria For Performance Excellence (CPE)

In your response, include answers to the following questions:

a. Product Offerings and Customer Support

1. **Product Offerings:** How do you determine product offerings? How do you:
   - Determine customer and market needs and requirements for product offerings and services?
   - Identify and adapt product offerings to meet the requirements and exceed the expectations of your customer groups and market segments?
   - Identify and adapt product offerings to enter new markets, to attract new customers, and to create opportunities to expand relationships with current customers, as appropriate?

2. **Customer Support:** How do you enable customers to seek information and support? How do you enable them to conduct business with you? What are your key means of customer support, including your key communication mechanisms? How do they vary for different customers, customer groups, or market segments? How do you:
   - Determine your customers' key support requirements?
   - Deploy these requirements to all people and processes involved in customer support?

3. **Customer Segmentation:** How do you determine your customer groups and market segments? How do you:

- Use information on customers, markets, and product offerings to identify current and anticipate future customer groups and market segments?

- Consider competitors' customers and other potential customers and markets in this segmentation?

- Determine which customers, customer groups, and market segments to emphasize and pursue for business growth?

Notes:

3.2. *Customer engagement* refers to your customers' investment in or commitment to your brand and product offerings. Characteristics of engaged customers include retention, brand loyalty, willingness to make an effort to do business—and increase their business—with you, and willingness to actively advocate for and recommend your brand and product offerings.

3.2a. *Product offerings* refer to the goods and services that you offer in the marketplace. In identifying product offerings, you should consider all the important characteristics of products and services and their performance throughout their full life cycle and the full consumption chain. The focus should be on features that affect customers' preference for and loyalty to you and your brand—for example, features that differentiate your products from competing offerings or other organizations' services. Those features might include price, reliability, value, delivery, timeliness, product customization, ease of use, requirements for the use and disposal of hazardous materials, customer or technical support, and the sales relationship. Key product features might also take into account how transactions occur and factors such as the privacy and security of customer data. Your results on performance relative to key product features should be reported in item 7.1, and those for customer perceptions and actions (outcomes) should be reported in item 7.2.

3.2a(2). The goal of customer support is to make your organization easy to do business with and responsive to your customers' expectations.

NIST (2015–2016) pp. 14–15

Baldrige in Plain English— Product Offerings and Customer Support

In the Organizational Profile (P.1b[2]) the Criteria for Performance Excellence (CPE) asks who the customer groups are and their requirements. Customer groups (*segments*) are determined based on the customers' requirements (customers with similar requirements are put into one customer group), as discussed in Area 3.2a(3). *Target* customer groups are based on how you sell to your customers.

In some instances you may need to group your product offerings the same way your industry groups theirs or you will not have comparison or benchmark data to evaluate your own performance.

Product Offerings

Within these groupings, the Criteria asks how you identify the product offerings that will meet or exceed the needs and expectations of customers, and how you innovate those offerings. The CPE expects the organization to have a wide view of customers, including the consideration of customers of competitors, other potential customers, and previous customers of the organization.

Once you determine the customer and market needs, how do you identify and adapt your product offerings to meet the requirements and exceed expectations? Beyond this level of adaptation, how do you adapt the offerings to new markets, new customers, and to create new opportunities to expand relationships?

These product offerings and the innovations should be structured so they provide opportunities to expand the relationship with the existing customers.

In simple terms:

- How do you *group* your customers? (segmenting based on their requirements)
  - How do you *sell* to those requirements? (your customer targeting)
    - How do you *deliver* to those requirements? (your facilities)

Customer Support

In the overall relationship with the external customer, the CPE asks how the organization determines the key mechanisms needed to support the customer's use of the products and the access mechanisms for customers so that they can reach the organization whenever they need to seek information, conduct business, or complain. For example, many organizations provide 800 numbers, 24 x 7 hotlines, or, in the case of key customers, the home phone numbers of key customer contact employees. The first step in this process is to determine the key customers' contact requirements—how do they want to be contacted and how do they want to contact the organization.

The CPE recognizes that each customer and customer group may have different contact requirements and different contact preferences. Some customers may wish to be contacted routinely, while others may wish to be left alone. How does the organization determine these customer preferences, and how does it ensure that all customer contact employees know these preferences? Quite frankly, this is a frequent shortcoming of many organizations. If you wish to have a relationship with a customer, you need to start with how they prefer to be contacted.

Another inherent part of this is how to train key customer contact employees. Although the Criteria is not explicit on this training requirement, it is difficult for customer contact to be systematic or for customer contact employees to help "increase loyalty and repeat business and to gain positive referrals" if customer contact employees do not systematically (and consistently) receive the necessary training and knowledge reinforcement. In many organizations, however, some key customer contact groups are overlooked. For example, the executives and support staff may not be included in customer contact training even though they often have frequent contact with customers. Executives, by virtue of their position, often feel as though they already have the customer skills and knowledge required. Additionally, support staff members often spend a great deal of time in direct contact with customers, even if they are not always viewed as critical to the customer response chain and may not be trained in customer contact.

In this item, the CPE attempts to assess whether the organization understands what drives their customers' purchase behaviors. Simply stated, if the organization truly understands what drives customers' purchase behaviors, it can compete more effectively in the marketplace than if it does not.

Finally, Area to Address 3.2a seeks to understand how the organization uses the information and data from its listening and learning methods (and analysis performed) to identify when and how product offerings need to be updated or new products developed.

Customer Segmentation

In the Organizational Profile (P.1b[2]) the CPE asks who the customer groups are and what their requirements are. These customer requirements should be segmented by customer group, target customer segment, or market segment, as appropriate. Item 3.1 asks how the organization systematically listens to those segments and appropriate groupings to determine the drivers of customer satisfaction, customer loyalty, and customer engagement. This listening must include obtaining feedback on your products, services, and customer support. Listening may be different for each customer group and should be tailored for each group. There are certainly instances where tailoring the listening approach does not make sense, but typically there are many more instances where it does make sense. The listening methods need to be broader than the organization's current customers. For example, the organization can learn from listening to former customers, customers of competitors, and potential customers. Their requirements may expand the organization's view of what is needed, or what is possible.

3.2b CUSTOMER RELATIONSHIPS

> *The customer doesn't expect everything will go right all the time; the big test is what you do when things go wrong.*
>
> SIR COLIN MARSHALL

 The Criteria For Performance Excellence (CPE)

In your response, include answers to the following questions:

b. Customer Relationships

1. **Relationship Management:** How do you build and manage customer relationships? How do you market, build, and manage relationships with customers to:
   - Acquire customers and build market share?
   - Manage and enhance your brand image?
   - Retain customers, meet their requirements, and exceed their expectations in each stage of the customer life cycle?
   - Increase their engagement with you?

How do you leverage social media to enhance customer engagement and relationships with your organization?

2. **Complaint Management:** How do you manage customer complaints? How do you resolve complaints promptly and effectively? How does your management of customer *complaints* enable you to recover your customers' confidence, enhance their satisfaction and engagement, and avoid similar complaints in the future?

Notes:

3.2b. Building customer relationships might include developing partnerships or alliances with customers.

3.2b(1). Brand management is generally associated with marketing to improve the perceived value of your product or brand. Successful brand management builds customer loyalty and positive associations, and it protects your brand and intellectual property.

NIST (2015–2016) pp. 14–15

Baldrige in Plain English— Customer Relationships

One of the key responsibilities of senior leadership is to create a customer-focused culture. If customers are not important to the senior leaders, why should they be important to anybody else? Check the leader's calendar—do they spend time with customers?

Years ago I remember sitting in a senior leader's office and hearing him say "At my level, I don't meet with customers. The leaders who report to me meet with them." I held my breath for several reasons: 1) he certainly was not role-modeling building a customer-focused culture. If customers were not important to him, why should they be important to anybody else in his organization? 2) How did he know what the customers really wanted? 3) He was viewing the customer relationship as a spectator sport and not a contact sport. 4) His corporate CEO (three levels up from him) spent 25% of his time with customers!

A customer-focused culture is composed of several organizational competencies: 1) understanding what the customer wants and needs; 2) consistently delivering what the customers want; 3) engaging the customers to understand your performance now and what will happen in their environment in the future; 4) aligning the culture and individual performance with the customers' interests; and 5) systematically building relationships with customers.

Relationship Management

With these foundational processes in-place, the organization needs to be able to build and manage relationships with existing customers in order to:

- Acquire new customers
- Build market share
- Retain customers
- Meet their requirements
- Exceed their expectations
- Increase their engagement with you

This needs to be done systematically in each stage of the customer and product or service life cycle. Through these processes, the organization should be able to increase customer satisfaction by meeting the customer's stated and unstated requirements which, in turn, should drive customer loyalty, which should then drive customer engagement.

Complaint Management

The CPE asks how the organization uses the complaint system to drive customer engagement. A simple way to view complaints uses the following questions:

- Are all complaints (both formal and informal) captured?
- Once captured, is the complaint addressed?
- If the complaint is not addressed in a timely manner, is the complaint escalated within the organization?
- Is the complaint closed with the customer?
- Does the way the complaint is addressed and closed with the customer drive increase:
  - Customer confidence?
  - Customer satisfaction?

- Customer loyalty?
- Customer engagement?
- Are all parties (including suppliers, partners, collaborators, etc.) who contributed to the complaint aware of the complaint and responsible for correcting the root cause of the complaint? This should include:
  - Ensuring the responsible parties know about the complaint
  - Ensuring the responsible parties fix the root cause of the complaint
- Is the complaint data aggregated, analyzed, and used to drive improvement actions? For example, when added up several small complaints may constitute an overall concern that the company should address. Unless both formal and informal complaints are collected, aggregated, and analyzed, the smaller complaints may not reach the attention of the leaders who can initiate action.

Category 4—Measurement, Analysis, and Knowledge Management

4.1 Measurement, Analysis, and Improvement of Organizational Performance

4.1a PERFORMANCE MEASUREMENT

A strong conviction that something must be done is the parent of many bad measures.

DANIEL WEBSTER

The Criteria For Performance Excellence (CPE)

In your response, include answers to the following questions:

a. Performance Measurement

1. **Performance Measures:** How do you use data and information to track daily operations and overall organizational performance? How do you

    - Select, collect, align, and integrate data and information to use in tracking daily operations and overall organizational performance?

    - Track progress on achieving strategic objectives and action plans?

What are your key organizational performance measures, including key short-term and longer-term financial measures? How frequently do you track these measures?

2. **Comparative Data:** How do you select and effectively use comparative data and information to support operational decision making?

3. **Customer Data:** How do you use voice-of-the-customer and market data and information? How do you:

   - Select and effectively use voice-of-the-customer and market data and information, (including aggregated data on complaints, to build a more customer-focused culture and to sup¬port operational decision making, and

   - Use data and information gathered through social media, as appropriate?

4. **Measurement Agility:** How do you ensure that your performance measurement system can respond to rapid or unexpected organizational or external changes?

Notes:

4.1. The results of organizational performance analysis and review should inform the strategy development and implementation you describe in Category 2.

4.1. Your organizational performance results should be reported in items 7.1–7.5.

4.1a. Data and information from performance measurement should be used to support fact-based decisions that set and align organizational directions and resource use at the work unit, key process, department, and organization levels.

4.1a(2). Comparative data and information are obtained by benchmarking and by seeking competitive comparisons. Benchmarking is identifying processes and results that represent best practices and performance for similar activities, inside or outside your industry. Competitive comparisons relate your performance to that of competitors and other organizations providing similar products and services. One source of this information might be social media or the web.

NIST (2015–2016) pp. 16–17

Baldrige in Plain English—Performance Measurement

In many ways measurement and information are the bloodstream that flows within the performance excellence model of any organization. Although Categories 1–6 focus on several hundred *hows* that require processes, these processes cannot be effective without performance measures. These measures must include both in-process and outcome (end-of-process) measures.

Performance Measures

Performance measurement begins with establishing the criteria that will be used to select performance measures and data. Many organizations have not consciously thought about this decision. Consequently, much of the data they collect and use evolves informally or is established on a case by case basis without clear decision criteria. The Criteria for Performance Excellence (CPE) model challenges the organization to take a more systematic approach, one that includes a repeatable selection process and explicit criteria for selection. The most basic *data selection decision* criteria are:

- Required data: Data may be required by regulatory agencies, governmental groups, higher level authority that may either be internal or external to the organization, the organization's policies, industry standards, or others. Simply stated, if an organization is required to collect specific data, then it should collect those data.

- Actionable data: By using this data, an organization can understand what actions need to be taken.

Other more complex data selection criteria can include the two criteria above plus:

- Data can be collected with integrity

- Data are easy to collect

- Data are meaningful to the owner of the data or the organization

- Data are understood by the users of the data

- Data are available at the source of the data or area to be monitored

Although data selection criteria are not specifically requested by the CPE (the Criteria question is "How do you select..."), answering this question allows an organization to more easily understand why it is collecting data and integrate its data collection process with how it actually uses the data.

Comparative Data

Another approach addressed in Area to Address 4.1a is how the organization collects, selects, and uses key comparative data. Most organizations attempt to drive a comparative mindset throughout the organization. They use comparisons not only at the highest level to make organization-wide decisions, but they also to make decisions at all levels.

Sometimes inexperienced examiners will write feedback to the organization that indicates that there should be a benchmark for virtually everything. This is usually impractical. Some comparisons are simply not available. The most important things to benchmark are the areas the organization must be successful at, as described in P.2a and P.2b in the Organizational Profile. If these are the factors that drive organizational success, then this is what the organization should fully understand through benchmarking.

Baldrige Award applications frequently discuss the organization's benchmarking processes. Few applications, however, describe the following components in their comparison selection and use process:

1. When the organization determines that performance (or other characteristic) is not what they wish
2. How the organization decides a comparison is needed
3. How the organization decides what data need to be compared
4. How the organization decides what other groups or organizations to compare against
5. The process the organization uses to collect comparative data (this is frequently called the *benchmarking process*)
6. How comparative data are analyzed once they are gathered
7. How the analysis is turned into an action plan
8. How the action plan is implemented
9. How performance metrics are monitored to ensure that desired changes are achieved
10. How corrective actions are taken if performance levels do not improve

The fundamental question in the above sequence is whether the data drive meaningful action.

Customer Data

The customer-focused organization starts with the senior leaders, in item 1.1. If they don't set a customer agenda, then it doesn't exist. Several places in Category 3 discuss the collection and use of customer-focused data. This part of the CPE asks how you select and ensure the effective use of the customer-focused data that you collect (including complaints). This includes how the data are used in strategic and operational decision making and innovation.

Measurement Agility

Once data have been gathered, analyzed and have driven improvement, the CPE ask how the performance measurement system is kept current with changing business needs. Once again, this systematic process needs to ensure that the organization's data collection, tracking, and decision processes can move at least as quickly as the external changes influencing the organization. This includes responding to unexpected organizational or external changes, and changing the measures accordingly. The key thought is that high performing organizations use data, analysis, performance reviews, and course corrections to respond to rapidly changing organizational needs. This ability makes the organization more competitive.

Once data are selected, collected, aligned, and integrated, leaders and employees throughout the organization need to use the data and information to support decisions. The CPE core value of *management by fact* is a key concept underlying Category 4.

4.1b PERFORMANCE ANALYSIS AND REVIEW

> *"Management" means, in the last analysis, the substitution of thought for brawn and muscle, of knowledge for folklore and superstition, and of cooperation for force.*
>
> PETER DRUCKER

The Criteria For Performance Excellence (CPE

In your response, include answers to the following questions:

b. Performance Analysis and Review

How do you review organizational performance and capabilities? How do you use your key organizational performance measures, as well as comparative and customer data, in these reviews? What analyses do you perform to support these reviews and ensure that conclusions are valid? How do your organization and its senior leaders use these reviews to:

- Assess organizational success, competitive performance, financial health, and progress on achieving your strategic objectives and action plans?

- Respond rapidly to changing organizational needs and challenges in your operating environment, including any need for transformational change in organizational structure and work systems?

How does your governance board review the organization's performance and its progress on strategic objectives and action plans, if appropriate?

Notes:

4.1b. Organizational performance reviews should be informed by organizational performance measurement, and by performance measures reported throughout your Criteria Item responses, and they should be guided by the strategic objectives and action plans you identify in Category 2. The reviews might also be informed by internal or external Baldrige assessments.

4.1b. Performance analysis includes examining performance trends; organizational, industry, and technology projections; and comparisons, cause-effect relationships, and correlations. This analysis should support your performance reviews, help determine root causes, and help set priorities for resource use. Accordingly, such analysis draws on all types of data: product performance, customer-related, financial and market,

> operational, and competitive. The analysis should also draw on publicly mandated measures, when appropriate.
>
> NIST (2015–2016) pp. 16–17

Baldrige in Plain English— Performance Analysis and Review

Once performance measurement and data selection (as described in 4.1a) are completed, analysis is used as the tool to translate raw data into actions. The CPE addresses this analysis at the most senior level of the organization because senior leaders review organizational performance and take actions that can impact the achievement of the organization's strategic plans. Nevertheless, high-performing organizations also have the ability to perform similar analysis at every organizational level.

While the CPE focuses on the highest levels of the organization, it does ask how the results of those analyses are deployed to the work group and functional levels within the organization so that every level of the organization can effectively support the decisions made at higher levels. Performance analysis is the key tool to translate data into usable or actionable information. The organization needs to then use this information to help drive actions to improve.

Once performance is measured and the results are analyzed, the Criteria asks how organizational performance is reviewed, and how senior leaders participate and use the reviews to

- Assess:
  - Organizational success
  - Competitive performance
  - Progress on achieving strategic objectives and action plans
- Respond rapidly to:
  - Organizational needs
  - Challenges in your operating environment
  - Need for transformational change in organizational structure and work systems

In high-performing organizations, however, the senior leaders spend the majority of their time on *changing the business* and not *running the business*. Sure, those senior leaders review performance and make course corrections. They are intimately familiar with the current performance of the organization, and may spend one or two days a week reviewing the past performance. That is not, however, where they spend the majority of their time. The *change the business* activities may absorb up to 80% of a senior leader's time in a high-performing organization.

4.1c PERFORMANCE IMPROVEMENT

> *Become addicted to constant and never-ending self improvement.*
>
> ANTHONY J. D'ANGELO

 The Criteria For Performance Excellence (CPE)

> In your response, include answers to the following questions:
>
> c. Performance Improvement
>
> 1. **Best Practices:** How do you share best practices in your organization? How do you identify organizational units or operations that are high performing? How do you identify their best practices for sharing and implement them across the organization, as appropriate?
>
> 2. **Future Performance:** How do you project your organization's future performance? How do you use findings from performance reviews (addressed in 4.1b) and key comparative and competitive data in projecting future performance? How do you reconcile any differences between these projections of future performance and performance projections developed for your key action plans (addressed in 2.2a[6])?
>
> 3. **Continuous Improvement and Innovation:** How do you use findings from performance reviews (addressed in 4.1b) to develop priorities for continuous improvement and opportunities for innovation? How do you deploy these priorities and opportunities:

- To work group and functional-level operations?
- When appropriate, to your suppliers, partners, and collabora¬tors to ensure organizational alignment?

Notes:

NIST (2015–2016) pp. 16–17

 Baldrige in Plain English— Performance Improvement

Once the performance measures are identified, data collected and analyzed and reviewed, the next thing to ask is how does this process help improve the organization? The CPE focuses on three aspects of improvement: best practice sharing, future performance, and continuous improvement and innovation.

Best Practices

Sharing best practices within the organization leverages lessons learned in one part of the organization to improve the entire organization. This means if one group improves, it also has the systematic ability to share it with others who can benefit from the improvement. This ability to share can be initiated during performance reviews when one group performs better than others. It simply is not acceptable to outperform your peers and not do something to help them systematically get better by using the techniques you found to be helpful.

Ideally, the performance review process and improvement projects include a step that requires sharing of the gain.

Future Performance

The ability to project future results should be included along with the performance reviews. Some high-performing organizations report the current results but also project the performance for each key metric at the end of the evaluation period. This helps them to understand the cyclicality of the business and what actions need to be taken to achieve the final desired results. This can help keep the organization focused during a high-performing period, and ensure that the organization does not become complacent if a down cycle is predictable. In both cases, the organization's progress toward a goal may not be linear, and the cycles incurred need to be understood and adjusted for with appropriate plans and actions.

Continuous Improvement and Innovation

The CPE also asks how the organization translates the performance review findings into priorities for continuous (ongoing) and breakthrough improvements. This process to translate the reviews into improvement actions should be visible in the senior leadership meeting notes. Do they ask for analysis? Do they ask for action to be taken? Do they understand the level at which breakthroughs have to be supported? Do they drive continuous improvement to all levels of the organization?

The Criteria also asks how the leaders foster innovation and the alignment of these reviews and the related actions and course corrections with suppliers and partners. This, as with all other aspects of the organizational focus, needs to be done through a systematic process. This process should typically start externally with the customer listening and learning posts, which should tell the organization how much innovation is expected, wanted, or needed.

4.2 *Knowledge Management, Information, and Information Technology*

4.2a ORGANIZATIONAL KNOWLEDGE

> *Everybody gets so much information all day long that they lose their common sense.*
>
> GERTRUDE STEIN

The Criteria For Performance Excellence (CPE)

In your response, include answers to the following questions:

a. Organizational Knowledge

1. **Knowledge Management:** How do you manage organizational knowledge? How do you
   - Collect and transfer workforce knowledge?
   - Blend and correlate data from different sources to build new knowledge?

- Transfer relevant knowledge from and to customers, suppliers, partners, and collaborators

- Assemble and transfer relevant knowledge for use in your innovation and strategic planning processes?

2. **Organizational Learning:** How do you use your knowledge and resources to embed learning in the way your organization operates?

Notes:

4.2a(1). Blending and correlating data from different sources may involve handling big data sets and disparate types of data and information, such as data tables, video, and text. Furthermore, organizational knowledge constructed from these data may be speculative and may reveal sensitive information about organizations or individuals that must be protected from use for any other purposes.

NIST (2015-2016) p. 18

Baldrige in Plain English— Organizational Knowledge

This focuses on the data, information, and knowledge management system to support the analysis/review of performance to improve organizational performance and share those improvements.

Knowledge Management

Managing organizational knowledge includes systems, collection of data, analysis, knowledge management, sharing of best practices, and decisions based on the data. These, however, cannot be effective if the data cannot be relied upon. This Area to Address focuses on being able to rely on the data. After several Baldrige recipients demonstrated an ability to leverage organizational knowledge for competitive advantage, knowledge management was officially added to the Criteria. In its ultimate form, knowledge management means anything that is known to one person in the organization should be usable by all people in the organization. Within that framework, the CPE asks how an organization collects and transfers employee knowledge. As with other parts of the CPE, a process with clear steps and decision Criteria needs to be employed. The two components of this process—collection and transfer—are handled separately by most organizations.

Some organizations have an excellent ability to collect data and develop world-class databases. In some cases, however, their ability to transfer it to the employees who need the data is insufficient. Clearly, the effective use of organizational knowledge to accomplish increased performance requires both collection and the use of knowledge.

The CPE also asks how the organization transfers relevant knowledge from customers, suppliers, and partners. This process is certainly more difficult across organizational, and often contractual, lines. As with any process, the examiners will be looking for the process steps, the decision criteria, and the metrics to know the process is a success. Most organizations collect best practices in some form. The CPE requires not only the identification of best practices, but effective sharing as well. Some high-performing companies have the ability to measure the impact of this sharing of best practices.

Organizational Learning

When an individual learns something, the CPE calls it Personal Learning. Organizational learning is achieved through research and development, evaluation and improvement cycles, workforce and stakeholder ideas and input, best-practice sharing, and benchmarking. Personal learning is achieved through education, training, and developmental opportunities that further individual growth.

To be effective, learning should be embedded in the way an organization operates. Learning contributes to a competitive advantage and sustainability for the organization and its workforce.

4.2b DATA, INFORMATION, AND INFORMATION TECHNOLOGY

Technology is dominated by two types of people: those who understand what they do not manage, and those who manage what they do not understand.

PUTTS LAW

The Criteria For Performance Excellence (CPE)

In your response, include answers to the following questions:

b. Data, Information, and Information Technology

1. **Data and Information Quality:** How do you verify and ensure the quality of organizational data and information? How do you manage electronic and other data and information to ensure their accuracy and validity, integrity and reliability, and currency?

2. **Data and Information Security:** How do you ensure the security of sensitive or privileged data and information? How do you manage electronic and other data and information to ensure confidentiality and only appropriate access? How do you oversee the cybersecurity of your information systems?

3. **Data and Information Availability:** How do you ensure the availability of organizational data and information? How do you make needed data and information available in a user-friendly format and timely manner to your workforce, suppliers, partners, collaborators, and customers, as appropriate?

4. **Hardware and Software Properties:** How do you ensure that hardware and software are reliable, secure, and user-friendly?

5. **Emergency Availability:** In the event of an emergency, how do you ensure that hardware and software systems and data and information continue to be available to effectively serve customers and business needs?

> **Notes:**
>
> **4.2b(2).** Managing cybersecurity (the security of electronic data) includes, for example, protecting against the loss of sensitive information about employees, customers, and organizations; protecting assets stored in the cloud or outside your organization's control; protecting intellectual property; and protecting against the financial, legal, and reputational aspects of data breaches.
>
> NIST (2015–2016) p. 18

Baldrige in Plain English—Data, Information, and Information Technology

Most of Area to Address 4.2b needs to be viewed from the user-of-data point of view rather than from the IT department's. User's needs should start (obviously) with the users. This, however, is not always the case. The IT department may feel they know what the users want/need or the users have what they need. The proof is whether or not the users have the right data at the right time, and the right access.

Data and Information Quality

Area to Address 4.2b(1) asks how an organization ensures the following properties of their data, information, and organizational knowledge: accuracy, validity, integrity, reliability, and currency.

To effectively address these characteristics, all solutions, which include practices and methods, must be designed to address the individual requirements. While some methods or practices may impact more than one characteristic, the details of how each is addressed should be explicit and clear. Unfortunately, organizations will often attempt to answer this part of the Criteria with a vague overarching statement that does not specifically address the processes, methods, and technology used to achieve each characteristic. Additionally, when answering this question, the differences between organizational data and information should be addressed.

Data and Information Security

This reviews how the organization manages electronic and other data and information to ensure that it is secure, confidential, and only the appropriate people have access. This includes ensuring cybersecurity.

Data and Information Availability

A critical part of the CPE is how the organization makes the needed data and information available to those who are involved with the organization. This should be addressed from the point of view of the users of data. Do they have what they need and how do you give them the access required? Making data available to the users of the data includes also making it available to suppliers, partners, collaborators, and customers, although they may need less data than internal employees need.

Data and information availability is the ability of the organization to put data and information in the hands of individuals who need it to run the business as well as those who are working to change the business. Ensuring data and information availability can include both automated and mechanical means so everyone has the data and information they need when they need it.

Hardware and Software Properties

Although IT may drive the processes to ensure that hardware and software are reliable, secure, and user-friendly, the ultimate judge of whether the organization is achieving its hardware and software availability and friendliness goal is the user's opinion. As such, this process needs to start with the user's requirements and end with the user's satisfaction.

Emergency Availability

How does the organization ensure that hardware and software will be available to those who are running the business (and to the appropriate suppliers and partners) in the event of an emergency? The simple question is, "Are our data and systems backed-up in case something happens?" Some organizations can answer this for their large systems, but do not have effective back-up for other types of data, which are manual or on portable computers. Both of these media can have critical data which would hurt the organization if lost.

Finally, how does the organization keep the data and information availability mechanisms current? This does not mean new equipment as much as it means focusing on the user's needs.

Category 5—Workforce

5.1 *Workforce Environment*

5.1a WORKFORCE CAPABILITY AND CAPACITY

An employee will give their all, as long as they feel valued and respected.

AMY ARMSTRONG

The Criteria For Performance Excellence (CPE)

In your response, include answers to the following questions:

a. Workforce Capability and Capacity

1. **Capability and Capacity:** How do you assess your workforce capability and capacity needs? How do you assess the skills, competencies, certifications, and staffing levels you need?

2. **New Workforce Members:** How do you recruit, hire, place, and retain new workforce members? How do you ensure that your workforce represents the diverse ideas, cultures, and thinking of your hiring and customer community?

3. **Work Accomplishment:** How do you organize and manage your workforce? How do you organize and manage your workforce to:

- Accomplish your organization's work?
- Capitalize on your organization's core competencies?
- Reinforce a customer and business focus?
- Exceed performance expectations?

4. **Workforce Change Management:** How do you prepare your workforce for changing capability and capacity needs? How do you:

- Manage your workforce, its needs, and your organization's needs to ensure continuity, prevent workforce reductions, and minimize the impact of such reductions, if they become necessary?
- Prepare for and manage periods of workforce growth?
- Prepare your workforce for changes in organizational structure and work systems, when needed?

Notes:

5.1. *Workforce* refers to the people actively involved in accomplishing your organization's work. It includes perma¬nent, temporary, and part-time personnel, as well as any contract employees you supervise. It includes team leaders, supervisors, and managers at all levels. People supervised by a contractor should be addressed in categories 2 and 6 as part of your larger work system strategy and your internal work processes. For organizations that also rely on volunteers, workforce includes these volunteers.

5.1a. *Workforce capability* refers to your organization's ability to carry out its work processes through its people's knowledge, skills, abilities, and competencies. Capability may include the ability to build and sustain relationships with customers; innovate and transition to new technologies; develop new products, services, and work processes; and meet changing business, market, and regulatory demands.

Workforce capacity also refers to your organization's ability to ensure sufficient staffing levels to carry out its work processes and successfully deliver products to customers, including the ability to meet seasonal or varying demand levels.

> **5.1a.** Your assessment of workforce capability and capacity needs should consider not only current needs, but also future requirements based on the strategic objectives and action plans you identify in Category 2 and the performance projections you discuss in 4.1c(2).
>
> **5.1a(2).** This requirement refers only to new workforce members. The retention of existing workforce members is considered in item 5.2, Workforce Engagement.
>
> **5.1a(3), 5.1a(4).** Organizing and managing your workforce may involve organizing the workforce for change as you address changes in your external environment, culture, technology, or strategic objectives.
>
> **5.1a(4).** Preparing your workforce for changing capability and capacity needs might include training, education, frequent communication, consideration of workforce employment and employability, career counseling, and outplacement and other services.
>
> NIST (2015–2016) pp. 19–20

Baldrige in Plain English—Workforce Capability and Capacity

Capability and Capacity

This area to address begins with identifying the capabilities (skills) the organization needs and how much of each capability is required (capacity equals the numbers of employees with the appropriate skill). The capability assessment can include the skills and competencies needed, and the capacity assessment can include the staffing ratios or levels. Key questions include: How does the organization assess their current workforce capability and capacity? How does the organization know what they are going to need in the future regarding workforce capability and capacity?

New Workforce Members

How does the organization find the right people and ensure they are brought on board? Once the organization determines what is required, how does it hire, develop, and keep the new employees? This can include new employee orientation and what some organizations call "on-boarding." Additionally, how do you ensure that your recruiting represents the same mix of ideas, cultures, and thinking of your hiring community? This view of diversity can be market-focused. For example, if your customer base has a wide range of backgrounds, experiences, needs, and expectations, you may need to have an employee base with that same diversity to be able to effectively serve your customers.

Work Accomplishment

How do you get the required work done? Once you have identified the needs and have the right employees on board, the CPE asks for a description of the process to manage and organize work to capitalize on the organization's core competencies. In simple terms, how do you get the right person and team doing the right work?

These individual competencies, and how they are applied to the work, should be managed in a way that drives a competitive advantage. Additionally, the CPE asks how the organization reinforces a customer and business focus, presumably at all levels of the organization, to exceed the performance expectations and goals at each level.

Finally, the CPE addresses how the organization integrates its strategic challenges (externally at the highest level) all the way down to detailed action plans, particularly as business needs change.

Workforce Change Management

How do you make changes as necessary, and prepare your workforce? As changes occur in organizational needs, particularly as they impact workforce capacity and capability, the organization needs to have a systematic process that addresses those needs and their impact on the workforce. Where the workforce size has to be changed—increased or decreased—there should be a process that can ramp up if capability and capacity needs to be increased, or minimize the impact of workforce reductions if the overall workload decreases. For example, many organizations use temporary employees to minimize the impact of a downturn. If the downturn occurs, they reduce the use of temporary employees to protect the jobs of their permanent workforce.

5.1b WORKFORCE CLIMATE

The superior man, when resting in safety, does not forget that danger may come. When in a state of security he does not forget the possibility of ruin. When all is orderly, he does not forget that disorder may come. Thus his person is not endangered, and his States and all their clans are preserved.

CONFUCIUS

 The Criteria For Performance Excellence (CPE)

> In your response, include answers to the following questions:
>
> b. Workforce Climate
>
> 1. **Workplace Environment:** How do you ensure workplace health, security, and accessibility for the workforce? What are your performance measures and improvement goals for your workplace environmental factors? For your different workplace environments, what significant differences are there in these factors and their performance measures or targets?
>
> 2. **Workforce Benefits and Policies:** How do you support your workforce via services, benefits, and policies? How do you tailor these to the needs of a diverse workforce and different workforce groups and segments? What key benefits do you offer your workforce?
>
> **Notes:**
>
> 5.1b(1). Workplace accessibility maximizes productivity by eliminating barriers that can prevent people with disabilities from working to their potential. A fully inclusive workplace is physically, technologically, and attitudinally accessible.
>
> NIST (2015–2016) pp. 19–20

 Baldrige in Plain English— Workforce Climate

This focuses on the work environment an organization creates for its employees. Is the environment safe and secure, and is the organization prepared for short- and long-term emergencies or disasters?

Workplace Environment

Baldrige applications frequently discuss the tracking of health, safety, and security issues on a reactive basis rather than taking proactive steps to prevent the safety issues. Proactive steps can include safety or ergonomics audits, security audits, health assessments, and tracking near misses. Near misses are incidents in which no one was hurt, but the potential for harm exists if the same circumstance occurred again. In other words, they were lucky. This is typically a leading indicator of future accidents.

Another aspect of work environment protection is how employees participate in improving the work environment and how the organization measures their performance. Additionally, the CPE asks for performance measures and the levels or targets the organization is attempting to achieve.

Workforce Policies and Benefits

In the Organizational Profile, an employee profile is requested. Differences in the needs of employee groups should be addressed. For example, if one group of employees is required to drive to customer locations and another group is not, the first group may have vastly different work place needs. Those differences should be clearly described. Tailoring to the needs of a diverse work force and different work groups and segments is critical. We must understand needs before we can effectively address them.

To accomplish this, high-performing organizations have listening posts to understand what policies and benefits are common or needed, a systematic process to determine whether a proposed policy or benefit is desirable from the organizational viewpoint, and finally, to determine whether the policy of benefit is good business.

5.2 Workforce Engagement

5.2a WORKFORCE ENGAGEMENT AND PERFORMANCE

The secret of joy in work is contained in one word - excellence. To know how to do something well is to enjoy it.

PEARL BUCK

The Criteria For Performance Excellence (CPE)

In your response, include answers to the following questions:

a. Workforce Engagement and Performance

1. **Organizational Culture:** How do you foster an organizational culture that is characterized by open communication, high performance, and an engaged workforce? How do you ensure that your organizational culture benefits from the diverse ideas, cultures, and thinking of your workforce? How do you empower your workforce?

2. **Drivers of Engagement:** How do you determine the key drivers of workforce engagement? How do you determine these drivers for different workforce groups and segments?

3. **Assessment of Engagement:** How do you assess workforce engagement? What formal and information assessment methods and measures do you use to determine workforce engagement, including satisfaction? How do these methods and measures differ across workforce groups, and segments? How do you also use other indicators, such as workforce retention, absenteeism, grievances, safety, and productivity, to assess and improve workforce engagement?

4. **Performance Management:** How does your workforce performance management system support high performance and workforce engagement? How does it consider workforce compensation, reward, **recognition**, and incentive practices? How does it reinforce:

    - Intelligent risk taking to achieve innovation?
    - A customer and business focus?
    - Achievement of your action plans?

> **Notes:**
>
> **5.2.** Understanding the characteristics of high-performance work environments, in which people do their utmost for their customers' benefit and the organization's success, is key to understanding and building an engaged workforce. These characteristics are described in detail in the definition of high-performance work (page 49).
>
> **5.2a(2)** Drivers of workforce engagement (identified in P.1a[3']) refer to the drivers of workforce members' commitment, both emotional and intellectual, to accomplishing the organization's work, mission, and vision.
>
> **5.2a(4).** Compensation, recognition, and related reward and incentive practices include promotions and bonuses that might be based on performance, skills acquired, and other factors. Recognition can include monetary and nonmonetary, formal and informal, and individual and group mechanisms. In some government organizations, compensation systems are set by law or regulation; therefore, reward and recognition systems must use other options.
>
> NIST (2015–2016) pp. 21–22

Baldrige in Plain English—Workforce Engagement and Performance

As Category 3 evaluated the customer segments, determined the requirements for each segment, and determined how the internal processes of the organization could be aligned to meet those requirements, Category 5 does many of the same tasks for the workforce.

Organizational Culture

Once the organization has determined the key factors in workforce engagement, the Criteria for Performance Excellence (CPE) goes on to ask how the organization establishes a culture that will effectively address those factors. Those factors should be aligned to drive high performance and a motivated workforce. Those factors include the ability to benefit from the diverse ideas, cultures, and thinking of the workforce. The CPE proposes that customers, partners, and collaborators have a wide range of experiences, needs, and expectations. Unless an organization has a workforce with this same breadth and depth, the organization may not be able to understand customer requirements or be able to meet needs in a way which will drive long-term performance or loyalty.

Once the above processes have been established to understand what drives workforce engagement, and to align the workplace to address those factors, the CPE asks how the organization empowers the workforce.

Elements of Engagement

The logic flow of workforce engagement begins in Area 5.2a, which asks how the organization systematically determines the key factors that will encourage workforce engagement. Although workforce loyalty is not specifically discussed in the CPE, loyalty should be assumed to be included as a step along the way to engagement. The results for workforce loyalty factors, such as absenteeism and voluntary turnover, are reported in item 7.3 Workforce—Focused Results.

Area 5.2a asks what *process* the organization uses to determine the different needs, requirements, and satisfaction and engagement factors for the various workforce groups or segments that were reported in the Organizational Profile.

Assessment of Engagement

This assessment of engagement can be a combination of both formal and informal assessment methods. Regardless of whether they are formal or informal, the organization should work toward developing as objective and quantifiable methods as is possible and practical. If these assessment methods differ across workforce groups and segments, the process to define these differences should be clearly described. It is acceptable for one process to be used for all workforce groups or different processes to be used for each workforce group. In either case, the CPE asks why that decision was made and the process steps for making the decision.

Where there are other indicators such as workforce retention, absenteeism, grievances, safety, and productivity, which give the organization insights into the workforce engagement, the processes to collect and use these indicators should also be described.

Performance Management

The workforce performance management system needs to be a systematic process that focuses on enabling and driving high performance work and workforce engagement. The process may be different for different workforce segments and different levels in the organization, but all workforce segments should: (a) understand what is required of them;

(b) understand their own goals; (c) understand their performance against those goals; (d) understand course correction and adjustments as they are made and the impact of these on their goals and actions; and (e) understand the linkage of their performance to compensation, reward, recognition, and incentives. Finally, the workforce performance management system should systematically reinforce a customer and business focus as it aligns action plans with the overall organizational goals and objectives.

The CPE specifically seeks to understand how the organization's Performance Management System supports:

- High performance work
- Workforce engagement
- Workforce compensation, reward (note: this does not have *to* be only monetary), recognition, and incentive practices
- Intelligent risk taking to achieve innovation
- A customer focus
- A business focus
- The achievement of action plans

Not only does the performance management system need to be linked to the organization's goals (as discussed in item 2.2), but it also should be linked to the overall development and growth of employees. Once employees clearly understand their goals and objectives, have the tools to perform, and have the leadership support, the performance management system should link and align compensation, recognition, and related rewards and incentive practices to the individual's and the team's performance.

Reward and recognition is an area in which most organizations have a tremendous opportunity for improvement. Even high-performing organizations can still improve further by more effectively aligning reward and recognition with the performance of the individual and aligning the performance of the individual with the objectives, goals, and direction of the organization.

Most organizations have some form of non-monetary reward and recognition, but this is typically an area of significant opportunity for improvement. As organizations increase the alignment of their reward and recognition of employees, including increases in non-monetary reward and recognition, the impact can be significant in its favorable effect on overall organizational performance. In the end, the goal is to align every employee's efforts with the efforts of the overall company. The performance management system is one of the major tools used to achieve that alignment.

5.2b WORKFORCE AND LEADER DEVELOPMENT

A little learning is a dangerous thing, but a lot of ignorance is just as bad.

BOB EDWARDS

The Criteria For Performance Excellence (CPE)

In your response, include answers to the following questions:

b. Workforce and Leader Development

1. **Learning and Development System:** How does your learning and development system support the organization's needs and the personal development of your workforce members, managers, and leaders? How does the system:

    - Address your organization's core competencies, strategic challenges, and achievement of short- and long-term actions plans?

    - Support organizational performance improvement, organizational change, and innovation;

    - Support ethics and ethical business practices?

    - Improve customer focus?

    - Ensure the transfer of knowledge from departing or retiring workforce members?

    - Ensure the reinforcement of new knowledge and skills on the job?

> 2. **Learning and Development Effectiveness:** How do you evaluate the effectiveness and efficiency of your learning and development system? How do you:
>
>   - Correlate learning and development outcomes with findings from your assessment of workforce engagement and with key business results reported in Category 7?
>
>   - Use these correlations to identify opportunities for improvement in both workforce engagement and learning and development offerings?
>
> 3. **Career Progression:** How do you manage career progression for your organization? How do you manage career development for your workforce? How do you carry out succession planning for management and leadership positions?
>
> **Notes:**
>
> **5.2b.** Your response should include how you address any unique considerations for workforce development, learning, and career progression that stem from your organization. Your response should also consider the breadth of development opportunities you might offer, including education, training, coaching, mentoring, and work-related experiences.
>
> NIST (2015–2016) pp. 21–22

Baldrige in Plain English— Workforce and Leader Development

The concept of a performance management system (PMS) was discussed in Area to Address 5.2a. The PMS identifies areas for employee development that are inputs to the workforce and leader development system. The workforce and leader development system addresses how individuals improve, assesses their improvement, and integrates their improvement with their career progression.

Learning and Development System

The manner in which the workforce learning and development aligns to core competencies, strategic challenges, and goals and objectives should be deployed all the way down to the short- and longer-term action plans. Additionally, workforce development should consider:

- Organizational core competencies, strategic challenges and achievement of:
  - Short-term plans
  - Long-term plans
- Organizational performance improvement
- Organizational change
- Innovation
- Ethics and ethical business practices
- Customer focus
- The transfer of knowledge from departing or retiring workforce members
- The reinforcement of new knowledge and skills on the job

One of the above questions asks how knowledge is transferred from departing or retiring workers. As with other aspects of the Criteria, this should be achieved through the use of a systematic process.

Leader development follows many of the same basic tenets of workforce development such as identifying core competencies, tying development to organizational performance, and ensuring that breadth and depth of development needed is achieved. In addition, leadership development should align with other parts of an organization, such as the leadership system discussed in item 1.1. First, each of the characteristics in the leadership system must be a part of the leadership development process and the characteristics expected in leaders should be a part of the leadership evaluations. If not, leaders will not know how to lead in a consistent way and will not think that the leadership attributes described in the leadership system are expectations of their personal leadership style. Second, leaders must be taught to develop people and taught to develop the processes (organizational learning) within their span of control. Finally, leaders must be role models at all levels. If the leader is not a role model, then those individuals who look up to that leader will not feel they are expected to act as role models either.

Learning and Development Effectiveness

Once the training of the workforce and leadership is accomplished, the organization has a responsibility to evaluate the effectiveness of the development and learning systems. This can be not only the impact on the individuals trained, but can also be the impact on the organizational performance. That linkage and impact are quantified in some high-performing organizations. Typically organizations will, at a minimum, ask for the reactions and feedback of those who attended the training. Some organizations actually assess the learning that took place through tests and examinations. It is one thing to have knowledge and another to be able to apply that knowledge on the job. Consequently, some organizations assess the impact of training to performance on the job. Finally, the most advanced organizations link the impact to performance on the job with overall enterprise performance measures associated with the overall strategy. The cost in both time and money increases as the organization implements more advanced assessment methods. Consequently, some organizations use the more expensive methods for only a few key or expensive training events. For more on the four levels of assessment search the internet on the key words *Kirkpatrick Model*.

Career Progression

The organization has a responsibility to help employees manage their career progression. This does *not* mean that every employee should have an explicit career path mapped out, including their next three positions. Most organizations have found that to be a low value-added activity. This is however, common in some technical paths, such as the steps of a nursing ladder as nurses develop in tenure and skill. What it does mean, however, is that for the highest levels of the organization, succession plans should be in place, with the associated development plans for each of the leaders on the succession plan. At all levels, employees should have the following knowledge of their job, their performance, and their potential:

- An understanding of their current job requirements
- An understanding of their current performance versus their job requirements (and the gap)
- An ability to receive the education, training, or experience to close the gap
- An understanding of the difference between their current job performance and the job they desire (and the gap)
- An ability to receive the education, training, or experience to close the gap
- An understanding and belief that once they receive the training, education, or experience required for the job they desire that the job selection process will be fair

Employee education, training, and development should link to the organization's strategic plan. The impact of people and employee capabilities were considered in the early stages of developing the strategic plan. The human resource plan was considered during the deployment of the strategy into action plans, leaving this portion of the CPE to address the specific development and training of leaders and the workforce to implement those plans. This plan begins with aggregating the training requirements at the highest levels in the organization so that the organization can directly link education and training to the achievement of action plans. The overall training and development plans must be deployed throughout the organization to link and align individual actions with short- and long-term organizational objectives.

The beginning of an employee's education starts with employee orientation. While no longer specifically required by the CPE, it is necessary if employees are to systematically learn the culture and necessary tools. This orientation should typically address the culture of the organization, the values and beliefs, and what employees have to do to grow into productive members of the organization. New employees should understand the same skills and tools that all other employees understand so that they can use those skills to solve problems, progress within the culture, or improve organizational performance.

Motivation and career development starts with the needs and expectations of the leaders and the employees and focuses on how the organization helps them achieve their development objectives through both formal and informal techniques. In the past few years, the CPE has asked about succession planning at all levels of the organization. Very few organizations truly plan for the succession of anyone except top leaders or those with critical skills. The Criteria now asks how the organization accomplishes effective succession planning for leadership and management positions. Nevertheless, the organization has the responsibility to ensure all employees have the opportunity to progress in their careers. The CPE now asks how an organization manages effective career progression for all employees throughout the organization. The organization should post all job openings so that eligible candidates have the opportunity to apply for all positions for which they are qualified and for which they have an interest.

Category 6—Operations

6.1 *Work Processes*

6.1a PRODUCT AND PROCESS DESIGN

Change is the process by which the future invades our lives.

ALVIN TOFFLER

The Criteria For Performance Excellence (CPE)

In your response, include answers to the following questions:

a. Product and Process Design

1. **Product and Process Requirements:** How do you determine key product and work process requirements? What are your organization's key work processes? What are the key require-ments for these work processes?

2. **Design Concepts:** How do you design your products and work processes to meet requirements? How do you incorporate new technology, organizational knowledge, product excellence, and the potential need for agility into these products and processes?

Notes:

6.1. The results of improvements in product and process performance should be reported in item 7.1.

> **6.1a(1).** Your key work processes are your most important internal value-creation processes. They might include product design and delivery, customer support, and business processes. Your key work processes are those that involve the majority of your workforce and produce customer, stakeholder, and stockholder value. Projects are unique work processes intended to produce an outcome and then go out of existence.
>
> **6.1a(2).** The potential need for agility could include changes in work processes as a result of overall work system changes, such as bringing a supply-chain process in-house to avoid disruptions in supply due to increasing external events triggered by climate change or other unpredictable factors.
>
> NIST (2015–2016) p. 23

Baldrige in Plain English— Product and Process Design

This area focuses on how the organization designs its products and key work processes, including the key design concepts and developing product and process requirements.

The term work process refers to how the work of your organization is accomplished. Work processes support the work systems discussed in item 2.1—Strategy Development. These involve your workforce, key suppliers and partners, contractors, collaborators, and the supply chain needed to produce and deliver your products and your business and support processes. For example, a health care organization may have inpatient, outpatient, and emergency *work systems*. Each of these *work systems* could be supported by the underlying *work processes* of:

1. Welcome patients
2. Register them
3. Diagnose their illness
4. Treat them
5. Educate them
6. Discharge them
7. Follow up after discharge.

Work processes coordinate the internal work processes and the external resources necessary for you to develop, produce, and deliver your products to your customers and to succeed in your marketplace. Decisions about work systems are strategic (Item 2.1 Strategy Development). These decisions involve protecting and capitalizing on organizational core competency and deciding what should be procured or produced outside your organization in order to be efficient and sustainable in your marketplace.

> Note: It is helpful to understand the definitions of systems and processes, and understand the difference prior to addressing the Category 6 Areas to Address. These can be found in the Glossary. Additional definitions critical to this understanding that are provided by the author but not supported by the CPE include: *Systematic Process, Enterprise Systems Model, Guidance Systems, Support Systems, blind spots*, and many others.

Over the years, the CPE has used several different approaches to describe the process management Category. This description has included terms such as *core processes, product and services processes, supplier processes, business processes, value creation processes, support processes*, and others.

- **Key Work Processes:** These are the key processes in the creation of products or services consumed by your external customers or those processes that are most critical to achieving your intended outcome.

- **Work Processes:** All processes. A subset of these is all other processes in the organization beyond the Key Work Processes. Sometimes the using organizations or, as some call them, the internal customers, refer to these processes as the "enabling processes." These processes support (or enable) other processes that produce the products and services for external customers.

Area to Address 6.1a asks how the organization designs its key work processes including design concepts and how it identifies the work process requirements.

Product and Process Requirements

Processes are a step where something occurs and have: 1) inputs; 2) outputs; 3) requirements; and 4) resources.

The overall work process requirements can start with inputs from the work systems, as well as customers, suppliers, partners, collaborators, and possibly others. The output of the process must meet what is expected by the customer of the process (the downstream process and the higher-level system). If it is a key work process, typically the customer will be external. If it is a support process, typically the customer will be internal. In both cases, however, the customer requirements must be systematically determined and the process must be designed to meet those requirements.

A clear understanding or picture of an enterprise system (key systems and their relationships) facilitates the identification of key work system requirements and the lower work process requirements. The key to clarity in this case is simplicity. In too many cases, the organization describes itself in terms so complex that nobody, either internal or external, can understand the key systems and processes, the inputs, outputs.

To describe the organization simply, the author recommends that an organization develop a one-page graphical description of its business, called an Enterprise Systems Model or *stadium chart*. (It's called a *stadium chart* because it describes the entire business as one view above the stadium.) This works for all sectors, including business, health care, and even government or not-for profit. This model can also be the basis for the organization's approach to process management. For example, the one-page description shows many of the key components of the business that can be broken-down further into the various levels of processes. These high-level systems can be broken down to the lower-level processes (typically broken down two or three more levels). See the Glossary for *Enterprise Systems Model*.

Design Concepts

This part of the CPE assumes that the overall work systems have been designed and the work processes within that system need to be designed. This is the level where actual work is performed. Additionally, the CPE wants the organization to understand how these processes contribute to delivering customer value. This presupposes that the customer value requested from the organization is aligned with the key work processes, which are aligned to the core competencies. To achieve the work necessary, every core competency should be addressed by one or more key work process to drive that core competency throughout the organization. Once the alignment of processes to delivering customer value is established, the processes must also drive profitability and sustainability as well as overall organizational success.

The first part of this area to address focuses on the product and work process design and key considerations. Work process design typically includes an analysis of the overall work system being supported, and the role of the process in that system. The first key consideration is how to design the products and work processes to help achieve and/or leverage the organization's core competencies. This was identified in the context section (Organization Profile). Core competency (ies) refer to the organization's area (s) of greatest expertise. These are those competencies that are strategically important and provide a sustainable competitive advantage in the market place or service environment.

These core competencies should have some alignment to the principal factors that determine the organization's success relative to its competitors (success factors). These factors were discussed in the Organizational Profile in item P2. The core competencies should also be linked to the organization's mission (for example, this is what we have to be good at to achieve our mission), competitive environment (for example, this is how you achieve a competitive advantage), and action plans (for example, this is specifically what you will do to achieve the competitive advantage). Anyone evaluating the organization would expect to see significant investments in improving or maintaining the capabilities within each of the core competencies.

6.1b PROCESS MANAGEMENT

> *Real success is finding your lifework in the work that you love.*
>
> DAVID MCCULLOUGH

The Criteria For Performance Excellence (CPE)

In your response, include answers to the following questions:

b. Process Management

1. **Process Implementation:** How does your day-to-day operation of work processes ensure that they meet key process requirements? What key performance measures or indicators and in-process measures do you use to control and improve your work processes? How do these measures relate to end-product quality and performance?

2. **Support Processes:** How do you determine your key support processes? What are your key support processes? How does your day-to-day operation of these processes ensure that they meet key business support requirements?

3. **Product and Process Improvement:** How do you improve your work processes to improve products and performance and reduce variability?

Notes:

6.1b(2). Your key support processes should support your value-creation processes. They might support leaders and other workforce members engaged in product design and delivery, customer interactions, and business and enterprise management.

6.1b(3). To improve process performance and reduce variability, you might implement approaches such as a Lean Enterprise System, Six Sigma methodology, ISO quality system standards, PDCA methodology, decision sciences, or other process improvement tools. These approaches might be part of the performance improvement system you describe in P.2c in the Organizational Profile.

NIST (2015–2016) p. 23

Baldrige in Plain English— Process Management

This part of the CPE assumes that the key work systems have been identified (2.1a[4]) and designed (6.1a[2]), and those work processes have been focused on the core competencies of the organization. The question asked in 6.1b is "How are the work systems managed and improved?"

Process Implementation

The Stadium Chart (Enterprise Systems Model) should show the systems, how they relate to each other, how they leverage the core competencies, and how they delivery customer value. This presupposes that the creation and delivery of customer value is aligned with the key work systems that drive the achievement of the core competencies. Once the alignment of systems to delivering customer value is established, the systems must also drive profitability and sustainability, as well as overall organizational success.

How do you ensure that the work systems are managed and improved to deliver customer value and organizational success, as defined by the multiple stakeholders? Organizational success implies that the organization is sustainable—economical, societal and environmental. A high-performing organization must be high performing in all three areas.

Support Processes

The systems that drive customer value are work systems or key work systems, but these must be supported by at least two other types of systems. Systems that Guide (See *Guidance Systems* in the Glossary) and systems that Support (See *Support Systems* in the Glossary). These are not described by the Criteria for Performance Excellence (CPE), but are key to understanding the organization and an enterprise-wide view of the interrelationship of all systems. All systems are supported by lower-level processes. The support systems are supported by support processes, which the CPE does ask about.

The CPE asks how you 1) determine what your key support processes are, 2) their requirements, and 3) how you ensure that you meet their requirements on a daily basis. This is achieved by 1) understanding the needs of your work processes, 2) working with the internal customer of the support system to define the requirements, measures and deliverables, and 3) by tracking the metrics to ensure that they are being achieved (output measures) and that the processes are in-control (in-process measures).

Product and Process Improvement

In the Organizational Profile (P.2c) a question was asked: "What are the key elements of the organization's performance improvement system, including the evaluation and learning process?" This question feeds directly into Area to Address 6.1b(3), which asks how you improve your work processes to improve your work processes to improve products and performance and reduce variation. Better performance can include both continuous improvement and breakthroughs (see Area 6.2d) and can be improvement in any aspect of the organization. Typical areas for improvement include cost, cycle time, variation, schedule, and quality.

The improvements in the processes, however, should be improvements that the customer or the stakeholders of the process—both internal and external—value. As discussed earlier, all processes should have Process Owners—somebody who is responsible for the caretaking and improvement of the process. Also, the Process Owners should have the responsibility to define, measure, stabilize, and improve the process. In improving the work processes, specific tools should be used. This does not mean that the organization must use only one improvement tool. Where several tools are used, however, it should be clear where and why each tool is used.

To drive these improvements, there should be input from the users of the output from the process. Where conditions change, or where the user wants a change in the output, the process improvement should be responsive to those differences and keep the process current with the changing needs. Finally, where improvements are achieved, there should be a systematic process to understand who could learn from this improvement, and to ensure that the improvement is understood by those individuals or groups. Some high-performing organizations also track the value of the improvements made in this manner.

6.1c INNOVATION MANAGEMENT

Great leaders make it safe for others to innovate.

JORGE BARBA

The Criteria For Performance Excellence (CPE)

> In your response, include answers to the following questions:
>
> c. Innovation Management
>
> **How do you manage for innovation?** How do you pursue the strategic opportunities that you determine are intelligent risks? How do you make financial and other resources available to pursue these opportunities? How do you discontinue pursuing opportunities as the appropriate time to enhance support for higher priority opportunities
>
> **Notes:**
>
> **6.1c.** Your innovation management process should capitalize on strategic opportunities identified in 2.1a(2).
>
> NIST (2015–2016) p. 23

Baldrige in Plain English—Innovation Management

The Criteria itself (not including the notes and other portions of the Criteria booklet) mentions innovation 11 times as follows:

Organizational Profile

P.1b(3) Suppliers and Partners

P2a(2) Competitiveness Changes

Category 1—Leadership

1.1a(3) Creating a Successful Organization

1.1b(2) Focus on Action

Category 2—Strategic Planning

2.1a(2) Innovation

Category 4—Measurement, Analysis, and Knowledge Management

4.1c(3) Continuous Improvement and Innovation

4.2a(1) Knowledge Management

Category 5—Workforce Focus

5.2a(4) Performance Management

5.2b(1) Learning and Development System

Category 6—Operations Focus

6.1c Innovation Management ⇨ This Area To Address

Category 7—Results

7.1b(1) Process Effectiveness and Efficiency

Few topics are addressed so frequently in the CPE. When discussed with the Baldrige Office, they have stated that *innovation is both a process and a culture*. This dichotomy is clearly reflected in the Criteria. This Area to Address (6.2d) describes innovation as a culture (What is your process to *manage* innovation). Other parts of the CPE address it as a process (Area 4.2a[1]—where it states "assemble and transfer relevant knowledge for use in your innovation and strategic planning processes."

The CPE asks how you manage innovation and how does innovation come from the strategic opportunities, which are analyzed to determine the appropriate risks (called intelligent risks). Once a potential innovation is identified, the CPE asks how you make the appropriate resources available.

All innovations, strategic opportunities, and risks need to be effectively vetted to ensure that they are reasonable.

6.2 Operational Effectiveness

6.2a PROCESS EFFICIENCY AND EFFECTIVENESS

Opportunity is missed by most people because it is dressed in overalls and looks like work.

THOMAS EDISON

The Criteria For Performance Excellence (CPE)

In your response, include answers to the following questions:

a. Process Efficiency and Effectiveness

How do you control the overall costs of your operations? How do you:

- Incorporate cycle time, productivity, and other efficiency and effectiveness factors into your work processes?
- Prevent defects, service errors, and rework?
- Minimize warranty costs or customers' productivity losses, as appropriate?
- Minimize the costs of inspections, tests, and process or performance audits, as appropriate?
- Balance the need for cost control with the needs of your customers?

Notes:

NIST (2015–2016) p. 24

Baldrige in Plain English—Process Efficiency and Effectiveness

Although the Criteria focuses heavily on work processes, all systems and processes must be effectively designed, managed—meaning kept under control—and improved. Each of these phases must consider the overall control and outputs, both initially and long-term.

Cost Control

The work systems, work processes, and the other types of systems and processes (such as those used for *Guidance and Support*; see the Glossary for definitions) need to be designed to achieve what the customers and the stakeholders of those systems and processes require. This design must include controls on factors such as cycle time, productivity, and other efficiency and effectiveness factors. The overall focus can be described as cost, schedule, and quality. To do this, the design and operation of the systems and processes must prevent defects, service errors, and rework.

To minimize warranty costs, customer's productivity losses, inspection/test costs, and process/performance audits, processes and systems need to have in-process measures. Through the tracking of these measures, the systems and processes need to be kept in control.

The Criteria for Performance Excellence (CPE) is non-prescriptive and will never require a specific technique such as statistical process control (SPC), but having short-interval in-process measures are critical to not having to "inspect-in quality" after a product or service are provided.

The essence of this portion of the Criteria is control, not artificially reducing the number of inspectors or audits without a methodology of ensuring the appropriate characteristics are maintained upstream of the outcome measures for the systems or processes.

Furthermore, incorporating cycle time, productivity, cost control, and other efficiency and effectiveness factors into the design of the processes, the organization should have the ability to link those characteristics back to the customer listening and learning posts (as described in item 3.1a) to ensure that these flexibility and productivity factors meet customer and/or marketplace requirements.

6.2b SUPPLY-CHAIN MANAGEMENT

To the degree one company integrates its supply chain better, and continuously improves it more rapidly than its competitors... It creates a competitive advantage for itself and the entire chain.

MIKE KATZORKE

The Criteria For Performance Excellence (CPE)

> In your response, include answers to the following questions:
>
> b. Supply-Chain Management
>
> **How do you manage your supply chain?** How do you:
>
> - Select suppliers and ensure that they are qualified and positioned to not only meet operational needs but also enhance your performance and your customers' satisfaction?
> - Measure and evaluate your suppliers' performance?
> - Provide feedback to your suppliers to help them improve?
> - Deal with poorly performing suppliers?
>
> **Notes:**
>
> **6.2b.** Feedback to suppliers should involve two-way communication, allowing suppliers to express what they need from you.
>
> NIST (2015–2016) p. 24

Baldrige in Plain English—Supply-Chain Management

This area asks how the organization manages and improves work processes, including the supply chain. The way the supply chain processes are planned, managed, and improved should be as rigorous as if they were internal.

Once the internal and external processes are designed and aligned to the work systems, the questions are: "How does the organization implement the processes to ensure that all key customer and stakeholder requirements are met?" and "How does the organization ensure that the work processes are stable?" This refers to minimizing costs associated with inspection. If the processes are in-control then they do not have to be inspected as often. In addition, to keep the processes current, the processes should be able to incorporate new technology, new organizational knowledge (through knowledge management), and the level of agility or innovation required by the customers or by the marketplace.

As with the controls in item 6.1, these processes need to be extended to the supply base. Although some organizations do not rely on suppliers to a significant degree, most organizations cannot thrive without a healthy supply chain feeding them.

As one leader stated: "You no longer compete *company-to-company*, you compete *supply chain-to-supply chain*."

Supply-Chain Management

The CPE asks how you manage your supply chain. This is an area that over the years has gone in and out and in and out of the Criteria. For some organizations, the supply chain is pivotal to even short-term sustainability. For other organizations, it is not as significant and does not need to be as robustly addressed. Where a robust supply chain is critical to an organization, the following questions should be answered:

- How do you appropriately include your supply chain in your strategic planning process?
  - This is key since plans must be supported by the suppliers.
- How you determine when to buy and when to make?
- How you qualify the supplier and determine who to buy from?
- How do you track supplier performance?
- How do you help suppliers improve their performance?
- What do you do if a supplier is performing poorly?

6.2c SAFETY AND EMERGENCY PREPAREDNESS

Action springs not from thought, but from a readiness for responsibility.

G. M. TREVELYAN

 The Criteria For Performance Excellence (CPE)

> In your response, include answers to the following questions:
>
> c. Safety and Emergency Readiness
>
> 1. **Safety:** How do you provide a safe working environment? How does your safety system address accident prevention, inspection, root-cause analysis of failures, and recovery?
>
> 2. **Emergency Preparedness:** How do you ensure that your organization is prepared for disasters or emergencies? How does your disaster and emergency preparedness system consider prevention, continuity of operations, and recovery? How does your disaster and emergency preparedness system take your reliance on suppliers and partners into account?
>
> **Notes:**
>
> **6.2c(2)** Disasters and emergencies might be related to weather, utilities, or a local or national emergency. The extent to which you prepare for disasters or emergencies will depend on your organization's environment and its sensitivity to disruptions of operations. Acceptable levels of risk will vary depending on the nature of your products, services, supply chain, and stakeholder needs and expectations. The impacts of climate change could include a greater frequency of disruptions. Emergency considerations related to information technology should be addressed in item 4.2.
>
> NIST (2015–2016) p. 24

Baldrige in Plain English—Safety and Emergency Preparedness

Safety

The CPE wants to ensure that the workplace is safe, secure, and ergonomic. Specifically, it asks how you provide a safe operating environment, including prevention, inspection, root-cause analysis, and recovery.

The CPE asks how the organization ensures that its work systems and workplace preparedness is adequate to survive and operate during disasters or emergencies. This includes prevention, management, and continuity of operations and/or recovery. To ensure the overall operational (short-term) sustainability of the organization, the organization will require:

- People
- Critical skills
- Facilities
- Equipment
- Data
- Money
- Adequate supply chain availability
- Distribution channels

Emergency Preparedness

Without any one of these factors, the organization will not be able to either respond to an emergency and/or ensure ongoing sustainability. An organization needs to assess:

- Prevention of disasters or emergencies
- Management of disasters or emergencies
- Continuity of operations when a disasters or emergency occurs
- Recovery from a disaster or emergency

More strategically, the factors noted in 1.1a(3) address the longer-term sustainability issues. Although the Criteria does not cover all of these factors, it can serve an organization well to take an integrated view of Emergency Readiness and Preparedness. This will ensure that the organization does not look at one single aspect of Emergency Readiness. For example, most organizations have a comprehensive IT Disaster Plan. Although this may help the organization protect their data, the organization can still be crippled if a critical aspect of the Supply Chain cannot deliver crucial products or services. The key issue is protecting the stakeholders. For example, protecting the customers so they will receive the products or services from the organization, and protecting the employees so they will have ongoing employment.

Category 7—Results

7.1 *Product and Process Results*

7.1a CUSTOMER-FOCUSED PRODUCT AND PROCESS RESULTS

It is quality rather than quantity that matters.

SENECA (5 BC–65 AD)

The Criteria For Performance Excellence (CPE)

> Provide data and information to answer the following questions:
>
> a. Customer-Focused Product and Process Results
>
> What are your results for your products and your customer service processes? What are your current levels and trends in key measures or indicators of the performance of products and services that are important to and directly serve your customers? How do these results compare with the performance of your competitors and other organizations with similar offerings? How do these results differ by process types, as appropriate?

> **Notes:**
>
> **7.1.** Results should provide key information for analyzing and reviewing your organizational performance (item 4.1), demonstrate use of organizational knowledge (item 4.2), and provide the operational basis for customer-focused results (item 7.2) and financial and market results (item 7.5). There is not a one-to-one correspondence between Results Items and Criteria categories 1–6. Results should be considered systemically, with contributions to individual results items frequently stemming from processes in more than one Criteria Category.
>
> **7.1a.** Results for your products and customer service processes should relate to the key customer requirements and expectations you identify in P.1b(2), which are based on information gathered through processes you describe in Category 3. The measures or indicators should address factors that affect customer prefer¬ence, such as those listed in the notes to P.1b(2) and 3.2a.
>
> **7.1a.** For some nonprofit organizations, funding sources might mandate product or service performance measures. These measures should be identified and reported here.
>
> NIST (2015–2016) p. 25

Baldrige in Plain English—Customer-Focused Product and Process Results

These results measure how the organization performs against the external customer's requirements (as reported in Area P1b[2] in the Organizational Profile). Product and service results are the *proxies* for customer satisfaction, and if they are understood should correlate to customer satisfaction, loyalty, and engagement. Because customer satisfaction measures are often lagging, these product and service measures provide timely feedback to help manage internal processes. Considering the requirements identified in the Customer Focused Items (3.1 and 3.2), what product and service characteristics, if done well, will result in a satisfied customer? For example, the customer might define quality and on-time delivery with no defects as an important service characteristic. This customer request might translate into percentage delivered on-time, average variance of delivery times, and number of defects per product found during final inspection, all measurable by the organization. The product and service results should directly correlate with the customer's satisfaction results.

Customer satisfaction and purchase behavior are the ultimate measures of product and service quality; however, customer satisfaction (reported in 7.2a) often lags behind the actual delivery of the products and services (7.1a). Consequently, customer satisfaction is often not timely enough to be used to control the quality of the products and services. An organization needs early warning proxies for customer satisfaction. These proxies come in the form of tracking the organizational performance against the characteristics of the products and services that determine customer behavior. The process to determine these requirements are reported in item 3.1, and the requirements themselves are reported in the Organizational Profile in P1a(1). Data reported here should align to what was listed in the Organizational Profile for each customer requirement within each customer segment.

Health Care Criteria

In addition to the item 7.1 requirements noted above, the CPE for Health Care Criteria also asks, "What are your current levels and trends in key measures or indicators of health care outcomes ....."

Unfortunately, we have seen some health care applicants provide *only* health care outcomes and not the internal measures which respond to the Customer's (Patient's) Requirements shown in Area P1b[2] in the Organizational Profile. While these clinical outcomes are critical for any health care organization, they do not answer the full breadth and depth of what Area to Address 7.1a asks.

The answer to P1b[2] gives an organization the ability to understand how they are meeting/not meeting what is important to customers (patients), which should correlate to satisfaction, loyalty, and engagement. If it does not correlate, the organization does not fully understand the customer's requirements. Clinical outcomes alone cannot create this alignment.

7.1b   WORK PROCESS EFFECTIVENESS RESULTS

Change is the constant, the signal for rebirth, the egg of the phoenix.

CHRISTINA BALDWIN

The Criteria For Performance Excellence (CPE)

> Provide data and information to answer the following questions:
>
> b. Work Process Effectiveness Results
>
> 1. **Process Effectiveness and Efficiency:** What are your process effectiveness and efficiency results? What are your current levels and trends in key measures or indicators of the operational performance of your key work and support processes, including productivity, cycle time, and other appropriate measures of process effectiveness, efficiency, and innovation? How do these results compare with the performance of your competitors and other organizations with similar processes? How do these results differ by process types, as appropriate?
>
> 2. **Emergency Preparedness:** What are your emergency preparedness results? What are your current levels and trends in key measures or indicators of the effectiveness of your organization's preparedness for disasters or emergencies? How do these results differ by location or process type, as appropriate?
>
> **Notes:**
>
> **7.1b.** Results should address the key operational requirements you identify in the Organizational Profile and in Category 6.
>
> **7.1b.** Appropriate measures and indicators of work process effectiveness might include defect rates; rates and results of product, service, and work system innovation; results for simplification of internal jobs and job classifications; waste reduction; work layout improvements; changes in supervisory ratios; Occupational Health and Safety Administration (OSHA)-reportable incidents; response times for emergency drills or exercises; and results for work relocation or contingency exercises.
>
> NIST (2015–2016) p. 25

Baldrige in Plain English—Work Process Effectiveness Results

Once an organization has identified what the customers want, the next question requires identification of the necessary internal support products, services, and processes needed to enable the key outcomes. High-performing organizations have a strong ability to identify the internal indicators used to control and improve the key product and service processes. These internal process performance indicators are important to the organization, but very often the customer could not care less about them. For example, if it is completion time for the foundation or the frame of a home a customer has purchased, the customer does not care if the foundation is finished on time. They only want high quality and the house ready to move into when predicted. The builder, however, knows that the probability of the house being ready to move into on time is dramatically increased by finishing the foundation on time. Thus, completing the foundation on time would be an in-process measure that the builder might use to ensure they meet the end-of-process measures that are important to the customer.

Process Effectiveness and Efficiency

The products and services provided to external customers by an organization are outputs of the organization's system of processes, including the outputs of both the key work processes and all other processes. This Area to Address focuses on the predictors of product and service quality reported in 7.1a. Results reported should include the key measures for performance of the work systems, including productivity, cycle time, and other measures of process efficiency (in-process measures), effectiveness (end-of-process measures) and innovation (if valued by the customer of the process). It also is essential to report key output measures of internal processes that enable or support the processes that provide the products and services provided to external customers as well as output measures of the key work processes. These measures, as well as others, should be used to proactively manage the organization's processes and to evaluate their overall performance.

Emergency Preparedness

Results reported against emergency preparedness should include the key indicators and measures for the achievement of the planning and mitigation of workplace preparedness for disasters or emergencies. This should show the factors addressed as important in 6.2c(2)—Emergency Preparedness.

7.1c SUPPLY-CHAIN MANAGEMENT RESULTS

Amateurs discuss tactics, professionals discuss logistics.

NAPOLEON

The Criteria For Performance Excellence (CPE)

> Provide data and information to answer the following questions:
>
> c. Supply-Chain Management Results
>
> What are your supply-chain management results? What are your results for key measures or indicators of the performance of your supply chain, including its contribution to enhancing your performance?
>
> **Notes:**
>
> **7.1c** This requirement does not ask for levels and trends. The reason is that some significant supply-chain results may be either qualitative or not amendable to trending over time. Examples for suppliers could be training hours on new products or processes, knowledge-sharing activities, audit hours that vary by supplier experience or specification complexity, or joint process and product development. When appropriate, however, you should report levels and trends for results that are numeric and trendable.
>
> **7.1c.** Appropriate measures and indicators of supply-chain performance might include supplier and partner audits, just-in-time delivery, and acceptance results for externally provided products, services, and processes. Measures and indicators of contributions to enhancing your performance might include those for improvements in subassembly performance and in downstream supplier services to customers.
>
> NIST (2015–2016) pp. 25–26

Baldrige in Plain English— Supply-Chain Management Results

Once an organization has identified what the customers want, the next question requires identification of the necessary internal and *external* support products, services, and processes needed to enable the key outcomes. High-performing organizations have a strong ability to identify the suppliers they need, and to integrate those suppliers into the full supply chain. Without this ability, many organizations may be ignoring over 50% of their total cost. This means the suppliers must be effectively rationalized into the entire value chain, and become a seamless part of planning, deployment, management, and improvement.

Unless an organization truly understands the impact of suppliers, they may put their business at risk in a manner from which it is difficult to recover. For example, a strong trend in the United States has been to offshore many products and services. Studies have shown, however, that some of these outsourcing decisions have ignored factors which contribute as much as 20% of the total cost. Clearly these decisions can put at risk some of the key factors that drove the decision to outsource, and may even put the competitiveness of the organization at risk.

7.2 *Customer-Focused Results*

7.2a CUSTOMER-FOCUSED RESULTS

> *However beautiful the strategy, you should occasionally look at the results.*
>
> WINSTON CHURCHILL

The Criteria For Performance Excellence (CPE)

Provide data and information to answer the following questions:

a. Customer-Focused Results

1. **Customer Satisfaction:** What are your customer satisfaction and dissatisfaction results? What are your current levels and trends in key measures or indicators of customer satisfaction and dissatisfaction? How do these results compare with those of your competitors and other organizations providing similar products? How do these results differ by product offerings, customer groups, and market segments, as appropriate?

2. **Customer Engagement:** What are your customer engagement results? What are your current levels and trends in key measures or indicators of customer engagement, including those for building customer relationships? How do these results compare over the course of your customer life cycle, as appropriate? How do these results differ by product offerings, customer groups, and market segments, as appropriate?

Notes:

7.2. Results for customer satisfaction, dissatisfaction, engagement, and relationship building should relate to the customer groups and market segments you identify in P.1b(2) and to the listening and determination methods you report in item 3.1

7.2a(1). For customers' satisfaction with your products relative to satisfaction with those of competitors and comparable organizations, measures and indicators might include information and data from your customers, from competitors' customers, and from independent organizations.

NIST (2015–2016) p. 26

Baldrige in Plain English— Customer-Focused Results

How satisfied are your customers? Are they more satisfied today than they were yesterday? How satisfied are your competitors' customers? These three questions are the validation questions for how well an organization is creating and delivering products and services that meet and exceed customer expectations, as well as how that performance is viewed by customers. Immediate customer feedback, however, is often impractical. Thus, formal and informal tools are needed to assess the customers' level of satisfaction and the resulting loyalty.

Customer Satisfaction

The customer-focused results reported in 7.2a validate the performance of the organization from the perspective of the customer and sometimes from the perspective of the customer's customer. Regardless of whether the organization collects revenue for their services, provides the service free of charge, or uses tax dollars, the primary beneficiaries of the key work processes are, for the purposes of this area, the customers that are external to the organization.

Why measure the customers' perceptions and purchase behaviors? One reason is to validate the product and service measures (7.1a) used to determine the quality of the output of the key work processes. An organization determines customer requirements, translates those requirements into product and service features, then measures how well the products and services meet those requirements. An organization knows that they have truly understood the customer's requirements only after they have measured the satisfaction, dissatisfaction, and behavior of the customer (7.2a). These should be compared to the performance levels of your competitors and of other organizations providing similar products or services.

Customer Engagement

The ultimate objective is not just customer satisfaction. Customer satisfaction should lead to customer loyalty. If it does not, then the organization does not understand the customer's requirements (reported in 7.1a). An organization does not want happy customers who leave; they want happy customers who stay. These are known as loyal customers. Loyal customers can then become advocates for the organization's products and services. These are known as engaged customers. The data presented here should be reflective of the customer relationship building processes described in Area to Address 3.2b. As with most results, these should be compared to the performance levels of your competitors and of other organizations providing similar products or services.

7.3 Workforce-Focused Results

7.3a WORKFORCE RESULTS

Your most precious possession is not your financial assets. Your most precious possession is the people you have working there, and what they carry around in their heads, and their ability to work together.

ROBERT REICH

 The Criteria For Performance Excellence (CPE)

Provide data and information to answer the following questions:

a. Workforce Results

1. **Workforce Capability and Capacity:** What are your workforce capability and capacity results? What are your current levels and trends in key measures of workforce capability and capacity, including appropriate skills and staffing levels? How do these results differ by the diversity of your workforce and by your workforce groups and segments, as appropriate?

2. **Workforce Climate:** What are your workforce climate results? What are your current levels and trends in key measures or indicators of your workforce climate, including those for workforce health, safety, and security and workforce services and benefits, as appropriate? How do these results differ by the diversity of your workforce and by your workforce groups and segments, as appropriate?

3. **Workforce Engagement:** What are your workforce engagement results? What are your current levels and trends in key measures or indicators of workforce engagement and workforce satisfaction? How do these results differ by the diversity of your workforce and by your workforce groups and segments, as appropriate?

> 4. **Workforce Development:** What are your workforce and leader development results? What are your current levels and trends in key measures or indicators of workforce and leader development? How do these results differ by the diversity of your workforce and by your workforce groups and segments, as appropriate?
>
> **Notes:**
>
> 7.3. Results reported in this item should relate to the processes you report in Category 5. Your results should also respond to the key work process needs you report in Category 6 and to the action plans and workforce plans you report in item 2.2.
>
> 7.3. Organizations that rely on volunteers should report results for their volunteer workforce, as appropriate.
>
> 7.3a(3). Responses should include results for the measures and indicators you identify in 5.2a(3).
>
> NIST (2015–2016) p. 27

Baldrige in Plain English— Workforce Results

Process performance is important but seldom occurs without an engaged workforce. People measures are an important input and predictor of process performance and, in some situations, customer satisfaction. Included in this area might be indicators of employee satisfaction, learning, and performance. Are the employee results good? Are they getting better? How does this organization's employee results compare to its competitors or organizations in the same business? Are their employees more or less satisfied? Who is getting better faster?

Area to Address 7.3a measures the multiple aspects of the people component of the organization. Product and service quality measures are not the only proxies of customer satisfaction. Heskett, Sasser, and Schlesinger (1997) link key people measures such as capability, satisfaction, and loyalty with productivity and services quality, which is linked to customer satisfaction and, in turn, revenue growth. Others have a HR scorecard aligned with and supporting the overall organizational strategy.

Workforce Capability and Capacity

The organization needs to have a process to determine the skills required (capability) and the numbers of people required (capacity). The measures for these should reflect the results tracked from the process.

Workforce Climate

The culture described in the Organizational Profile (P.1a) and reflected in the Workforce Climate (5.1b) should be tracked in the results reported here. At a minimum, this should include the current levels and trends in key measures or indicators of health, safety, security, and services and benefits.

Workforce Engagement

The *people* results should be comprehensive enough to provide a clear picture of the overall status of the workforce and should also provide insight into the various segments of the workforce. As with the other measures discussed in this book, the human resource measures should include both leading and lagging measures. Measures should include how the organization knows the workforce is engaged and satisfied.

Workforce Development

The development of the workforce and the leaders should be reported. At a minimum, this includes leading and lagging measures of development. Measures should include how the organization knows the workforce is developing, increasing capability and capacity.

7.4 *Leadership and Governance Results*

7.4a LEADERSHIP, GOVERNANCE AND SOCIETAL RESPONSIBILITY RESULTS

Leadership is based on inspiration, not domination; on cooperation, not intimidation.

WILLIAM ARTHUR WOOD

The Criteria For Performance Excellence (CPE)

Provide data and information to answer the following questions:

a. **Leadership, Governance, and Societal Responsibility Results**

1. **Leadership:** What are your results for senior leaders' communication and engagement with the workforce and customers? What are your results for key measures or indicators of senior leaders' communication and engagement with the workforce and customers to deploy your vision and values, encourage two-way communication, and create a focus on action? How do these results differ by organizational units and customer groups, as appropriate?

2. **Governance:** What are your results for governance accountability? What are your key current findings and trends in key measures or indicators of governance and internal and external fiscal accountability, as appropriate?

3. **Law and Regulation:** What are your legal and regulatory results? What are your results for key measures or indicators of meeting and surpassing regulatory and legal requirements? How do these results differ by organizational units, as appropriate?

4. **Ethics:** What are your results for ethical behavior? What are your results for key measures or indicators of ethical behavior and of stakeholder trust in your senior leaders and governance? How do these results differ by organizational units, as appropriate?

5. **Society:** What are your results for societal responsibilities and support of your key communities? What are your results for key measures or indicators of your fulfillment of your societal responsibilities and support of your key communities?

Notes:

7.4. Most of the requirements in this item do not ask for levels and trends. The reason is that some significant results may be either qualitative in nature or not amenable to trending over time. Examples could be results of intelligent risk taking and governance accountability. For such results, qualitative explanation may be more meaningful than current levels and trends. When appropriate, however, you should report levels and trends for results that are numeric and trendable.

7.4a(1). Responses should relate to the communication processes you identify in item 1.1.

7.4a(2). Responses might include financial statement issues and risks, important internal and external auditor recom¬mendations, and management's responses to these matters. Some nonprofit organizations might also report results of IRS 990 audits.

7.4a(3). Legal and regulatory results should relate to the requirements you report in 1.2b. Workforce-related occu¬pational health and safety results (for example, OSHA-reportable incidents) should be reported in 7.1b(1) and 7.3a(2).

7.4a(4). For examples of measures of ethical behavior and stakeholder trust, see the note to 1.2b(2).

7.4a(5). Responses should relate to the societal responsibili¬ties you report in 1.2b(1) and 1.2c(1), as well as the support of the key communities you report in 1.2c(2). Measures of contributions to societal well-being might include those for reduced energy consumption, the use of renewable energy resources and recycled water, reduction of carbon footprint, waste reduction and utilization, alternative approaches to conserving resources (for example, increased audio and video conferencing), and the global use of enlightened labor practices.

NIST (2015–2016) p. 28

Baldrige in Plain English—Leadership, Governance and Societal Responsibility Results

While it is critically important to satisfy customers and empower the workforce, these measures are incomplete. Performance excellence is only sustainable if the organization is operating in a way that is consistent and in the interest of the communities in which it operates as well as the public at large. Consider the company that pollutes the town's water supply. Eventually, the reaction from the local community will make it difficult for the business to profitably operate. If the executives act unethically, trust with the employees, customers, partners, and investors will be destroyed. Without trust and support from these key stakeholders, the processes, no matter how fancy, will fail to produce sustainable results. This area focuses on how well the organization achieves a range of results. These aspects include:

- **Leadership:**
    - Communication
    - Engagement
    - Deployment of vision and values
    - Communication
    - Action focus
- **Governance:**
    - Governance
    - Fiscal accountability
    - Internal and external measures
- **Law and Regulation:**
    - Surpassing legal requirements
    - Surpassing regulatory requirements
- **Ethics:**
    - Ethical behavior
    - Stakeholder trust in senior leaders
    - Stakeholder trust in governance
    - Key indicators of breaches in ethical behavior

- **Society:**
  - Fulfillment of societal responsibilities
  - Support of the community
  - Contributions to community health (for the Health Care Criteria)

7.4b STRATEGY IMPLEMENTATION RESULTS

Leaders establish the vision for the future and set the strategy for getting there.

JOHN P. KOTTER

The Criteria For Performance Excellence (CPE)

> Provide data and information to the following questions:
>
> b. Strategy Implementation Results
>
> What are your results for the achievement of your organizational strategy and action plans? What are your results for key measures or indicators of the achievement of your organizational strategy and action plans? What are your results for building and strengthening core competencies? What are your results for taking intelligent risks?
>
> **Notes:**
>
> **7.4b.** Measures or indicators of strategy and action plan achievement should relate to the strategic objectives and goals you report in 2.1b(1) and the action plan performance measures and projected performance you report in 2.2a(5) and 2.2a(6), respectively.
>
> NIST (2015–2016) p. 28

Baldrige in Plain English—Strategy Implementation Results

This area to address focuses on the results achieved from the implementation of your action plans identified in Area to Address 2.2a. While improving results are reported in the trends throughout the results items 7.1 through 7.5, this area asks for results specific to the effectiveness of the action plans. These results include the projections provided in Area to Address 2.2b[1].

While one would expect the improvement trends related to strategy to be found in all Results areas, this area focuses on how well the organization achieves the results related to the implementation of the action plans identified in 2.2a and the related projections identified in 2.2b. These results include key measures or indicators of:

- The accomplishment of the organizational strategic goals and objectives—2.1a

- The accomplishment of the organizational action plans. This should be focused at the organizational level, or for key plans—2.2a and related performance projections—2.2b

- The building and strengthening of the organization's core competencies

The metrics shown can be a combination of both leading and lagging indicators. While these results are not the central purpose of the organization, they are essential aspects that determine overall success. An organization cannot succeed merely by performing well on these metrics. To perform poorly on one or more of these metrics, however, may spell disaster.

7.5 *Financial and Market Results*

7.5a FINANCIAL AND MARKET RESULTS

> *Poor is the man who does not know his own intrinsic worth and tends to measure everything by relative value. A man of financial wealth who values himself by his financial net worth is poorer than a poor man who values himself by his intrinsic self-worth.*
>
> SIDNEY MADWED

The Criteria For Performance Excellence (CPE)

Provide data and information to answer the following questions:

a. Financial and Market Results

1. **Financial Performance:** What are your financial performance results? What are your current levels and trends in key measures or indicators of financial performance, including aggregate measures of financial return, financial viability, and budgetary performance, as appropriate? How do these results differ by market segments and customer groups, as appropriate?

2. **Marketplace Performance:** What are your marketplace performance results? What are your current levels and trends in key measures or indicators of marketplace performance, including market share or position, market and market share growth, and new markets entered, as appropriate? How do these results differ by market segments and customer groups, as appropriate?

Notes:

7.5a(1) Aggregate measures of financial return might include those for return on investment (ROI), operating margins, profitability, or profitability by market segment or customer group. Measures of financial viability might include those for liquidity, debt-to-equity ratio, days cash on hand, asset utilization, and cash flow. Measures should relate to the financial measures you report in 4.1a(1) and the financial management approaches you report in item 2.2. For nonprofit organizations, additional measures might include performance to budget, reserve funds, cost avoidance or savings, administrative expenditures as a percentage of budget, and the cost of fundraising versus funds raised.

7.5a(2) For nonprofit organizations, responses might include measures of charitable donations or grants and the number of new programs or services offered.

NIST (2015–2016) p. 29

Baldrige in Plain English—Financial and Market Results

These measure the outcome of how well the organization produces products, delivers services, and creates a positive customer experience by measuring the customer's purchase behavior through revenue and growth. This also shows how well the organization can control its costs and thus its overall profit. When considered over the long-term, these provide a reasonably good indication of the organization's performance—at least for commercial for-profit organizations. These results include aggregate measures of financial return and economic value. For marketplace performance, these results also include market share or position, business growth, and new markets entered. This shows the combined effectiveness of the value creation processes (revenue) with the efficiency of the processes (expenses).

Financial Performance

By measuring expenses, financial measures also determine how efficient the organization is at creating and delivering products and services. Financial measures are the ultimate validation of both process effectiveness and efficiency. Like customer satisfaction, however, they are lagging measures and are often not so useful for managing the processes and people to ensure future organizational performance.

Marketplace Performance

This item also looks at marketplace performance. Is the market share growing or shrinking? Market share trends are rarely a stand-alone number. For example, if the organization has a dominate market share, they may be world-class in all that they do, but still not be able to hold their market share if enough competitors enter and/or if competitors take irrational actions such as dumping their products on the marketplace below their cost.

Glossary
Key Terms

This Glossary of Key Terms defines and briefly describes terms used throughout this book that are important to key performance management concepts. The majority of this glossary was taken directly from the Baldrige Criteria (NIST, 2015–2016, pp. 47–54). The definitions have been slightly edited and some definitions added for use with this book.

Where the term being defined is in italics (or where part of the definition is in italics), the italicized part of the definition has been provided by the author (or Wikipedia) and is not endorsed by the Baldrige Office.

Action Plans

The term "action plans" refers to specific actions that respond to short- and longer-term strategic objectives. Action plans include details of resource commitments and time horizons for accomplishment. Action plan development represents the critical stage in planning when strategic objectives and goals are made specific so that effective, organization-wide understanding, and deployment are possible. In the Criteria, deployment of action plans includes creating aligned measures for all departments and work units. Deployment also might require specialized training for some employees or recruitment of personnel.

An example of a strategic objective for a supplier in a highly-competitive industry might be to develop and maintain a price leadership position. Action plans could entail designing efficient processes and creating an accounting system that tracks activity-level costs, aligned for the organization as a whole. Deployment requirements might include work unit and team training in setting priorities based on costs and benefits. Organizational-level analysis and review likely would emphasize productivity growth, cost control, and quality.

Alignment

The term "alignment" refers to consistency of plans, processes, information, resource decisions, actions, results, and analyses to support key organization-wide goals. Effective alignment requires a common understanding of purposes and goals. It also requires the use of complementary measures and information for planning, tracking, analysis, and improvement at three levels: the organizational level, the key process level, and the work unit level.

Analysis

The term "analysis" refers to an examination of facts and data to provide a basis for effective decisions. Analysis often involves the determination of cause-effect relationships. Overall organizational analysis guides the management of work systems and work processes toward achieving key business results and toward attaining strategic objectives. Despite their importance, individual facts and data do not usually provide an effective basis for actions or setting priorities. Effective actions depend on an understanding of relationships derived from analysis of facts and data.

Anecdotal

The term "anecdotal" refers to process information that lacks specific methods, measures, deployment mechanisms, and evaluation, improvement, and learning factors. Anecdotal information frequently uses examples and describes individual activities rather than systematic processes. An anecdotal response to how senior leaders deploy performance expectations might describe a specific occasion when a senior leader visited all of the organization's facilities. On the other hand, a systematic process might describe the communication methods used by all senior leaders to deliver performance expectations on a regular basis to all organizational locations and workforce members, the measures used to assess the effectiveness of the methods, and the tools and techniques used to evaluate and improve the communication methods.

Approach

The term "approach" refers to the methods used by an organization to address the Baldrige Criteria Item requirements. Approach includes the appropriateness of the methods to the item requirements and to the organization's operating environment, as well as how effectively the methods are used. Approach is one of the dimensions considered in evaluating process Items.

Balancing Value

A key challenge to an organization will frequently include balancing the differing expectations of the various stakeholder groups. To meet the sometimes conflicting and changing aims that balancing value implies, organizational strategy, which is normally in the environmental scan phase of strategy development, should explicitly include key stakeholder requirements. This will help the organization develop strategies along with the associated plans and actions that are aligned to maximize the overall stakeholder benefit, and to achieve what the leaders of the organization intended to achieve.

This does not mean that all stakeholders will get anything they want. It does mean that the leadership needs to start with the stakeholders' requirements, and determine the most effective/innovative way to serve the needs of multiple stakeholders. During the planning, the balance intended by the leaders between the stakeholder requirements and how they will/will not be met) should be linked to the beliefs of the organization (for example mission, vision, values), and the needs of the multiple stakeholders. The balanced intended should be the balance planned, the balance resourced, the balance deployed, the balanced reviewed (during performance reviews), and the balance achieved.

Basic Requirements

The term "basic requirements" refers to the topic Criteria users need to address when responding to the most central concept of an item. Basic requirements are the fundamental theme of that item (for example your approach for strategy development for item 2.1). In the Criteria, the basic requirements of each item are presented as the item title question. This presentation is illustrated in the item format.

Benchmarks

The term "benchmarks" refers to processes and results that represent best practices and performance for similar activities, inside or outside an organization's industry. Organizations engage in benchmarking to understand the current dimensions of world-class performance and to achieve discontinuous (non-incremental) or "breakthrough" improvement.

Benchmarks are one form of comparative data. Other comparative data organizations might use include industry data collected by a third party (frequently industry averages), data on competitors' performance, and comparisons with similar organizations that are in the same geographic area or that provide similar products and services in other geographic areas.

Big Data

For all organizations, turning data into knowledge, and knowledge into useful strategic insights is the real challenge of big data. While the volume of data an organization must assimilate and use in decision making may vary widely, all organizations are faced with using data from different sources and of varying quality. This presents challenges in data validation, frequently exacerbated when the data being validated include numerics, text, and video or other formats. Organizations must deal increasingly with more sophisticated data analytics and issues of data integrity. Challenges to cybersecurity enhance the pressures on organizations and increase the need for organizational sophistication. User demands increase the need for speed and availability of data. In 2015, the Criteria incorporated an enhanced focus on data analytics, data integrity, and cybersecurity.

Blind Spot

The term "blind spot" refers to an area that is not being addressed by the organization, which is an obscuration of the visual field (or environmental scan) during the planning and implementation of actions. A particular blind spot is the place in the visual field that is not being addressed. If an organization does not address a blind spot, there is some level of risk to the organization or to organizational performance. A blind spot could potentially interfere with organizational performance and strategy.

Blind spots can be something the organization is unaware of, something they are aware of, or even something they understand. In any event, however, a decision to act to remove or mitigate the blind spot has not been made, and actions have not been taken.

Once a decision to act is made, the organization should monitor the progress of the actions to determine whether the intended effect of removing or mitigating the risk has occurred. If action is not taken, the organization may still want to monitor the blind spot to ensure the level of risk, which the blind spot represents, does not change to an unacceptable level. For example: known blind spots can be areas which the organization is aware of, but they have not taken action to mitigate the risk because of a conscious leadership decision that the risk is acceptable. Additionally, some known blind spots can be of a nature that the organization does not know what to do about them, or cannot do anything about them.

Areas of risk the organization is not aware of are called unknown blind spots. Frequently these are addressed with the use of specific external experts who can make the organization aware of risks that were previously unknown.

Change Management

Organizational change is difficult and generally disruptive to the organization and its people. It requires dedication and commitment. The strategic imperatives and decisions about change have been a focus of past updates to the Criteria. The roadblock many organizations face is that designing change is much easier than the dedication and commitment required to implement, fully deploy, and sustain change. Revisions to the 2015–2016 Criteria emphasize the ability to accomplish these tactical aspects of change.

Climate Change

While some organizations have a greater opportunity than others to contribute to eliminating the sources of climate change, no organization is immune to its impacts. This is true of all types and sizes of businesses, nonprofit organizations, and government entities. Increasingly severe storms, massive snows, flooding, and power outages potentially affect supply chains, the ability to work, productivity, and the ability to move around. These events increase the need for aid from social service and government agencies. For all organizations, the impacts of climate change are about managing risk, making choices, and building acceptable redundancies and alternatives into performance management systems, while not building overcapacity and wasteful systems. These contingencies are addressed in the 2015–2016 Criteria.

Collaborators

The term "collaborators" refers to those organizations or individuals who cooperate with your organization to support a particular activity or event, or who cooperate on an intermittent basis when short-term goals are aligned or are the same. Typically, collaborations do not involve formal agreements or arrangements. See also the definition of "partners."

Core Competencies

The term "core competencies" refers to your organization's areas of greatest expertise. Your organization's core competencies are those strategically important capabilities that are central to fulfilling your mission or that provide an advantage in your marketplace or service environment. Core competencies frequently are challenging for competitors or suppliers and partners to imitate, and they may provide a sustainable competitive advantage. Core competencies may involve technology expertise, unique service offerings, a marketplace niche, or particular business acumen, for example business acquisitions).

Customer

The term "customer" refers to actual and potential users of your organization's products, programs, or services (referred to as "products" in the Criteria). Customers include the end users of your products, as well as others who might be their immediate purchasers or users. These others might include distributors, agents, or organizations that further process your product as a component of their product. The Criteria addresses customers broadly, referencing current and future customers, as well as the customers of your competitors.

Customer-driven excellence is a Baldrige Core Value embedded in the beliefs and behaviors of high-performing organizations. Customer focus impacts, and should integrate, an organization's strategic directions, its work systems, work processes, and its business results.

Customer Engagement

The term "customer engagement" refers to your customers' investment in or commitment to your brand and product offerings. It is based on your ongoing ability to serve their needs and build relationships so that customers will continue using your products. Characteristics of customer engagement include customer retention and loyalty, customers' willingness to make an effort to do business with your organization, and customers' willingness to actively advocate for and recommend your brand and product offerings.

Customer Group

Customer groups might be based on common expectations, behaviors, preferences, or profiles. Within a group there may be customer segments based on differences and commonalities. For most purposes, the term "customer group" in the Criteria has replaced the term "customer segment."

Customer Segment

The term "customer group" in the Criteria has replaced the term "customer segment' in previous versions of the Criteria. See the definition of "Segment" and the definition of "Customer Group."

Cycle Time

The term "cycle time" refers to the time required to fulfill commitments or to complete tasks. Time measurements play a major role in the Criteria because of the great importance of time performance to improving competitiveness and overall performance. "Cycle time" refers to all aspects of time performance. Cycle time improvement might include time to market, order fulfillment time, delivery time, changeover time, customer response time, and other key measures of time.

Deployment

The term "deployment" refers to the extent to which an approach is applied in addressing the requirements of a Baldrige Criteria Item. Deployment is evaluated on the basis of the breadth and depth of application of the approach to relevant work units throughout the organization. Deployment is one of the dimensions considered in evaluating Process Items. For further description, see the "Scoring System."

Diversity

The term "diversity" refers to valuing and benefiting from personal differences. These differences address many variables, including race, religion, color, gender, national origin, disability, sexual orientation, age and generational preferences, education, geographic origin, and skill characteristics, as well as differences in ideas, thinking, academic disciplines, and perspectives.

The Baldrige Criteria refer to the diversity of your workforce hiring and customer communities. Capitalizing on both provides enhanced opportunities for high performance; customer, workforce, and community satisfaction; and customer and workforce engagement.

Effective

The term "effective" refers to how well a process or a measure addresses its intended purpose. Determining effectiveness requires: (1) the evaluation of how well the process is aligned with the organization's needs and how well the process is deployed, or (2) the evaluation of the outcome of the measure used.

Embedded Core Belief

A term used by some organizations to describe the one belief that is so key that it is at the top of every thought, process, plan, measure, and action. This is part of an organization's DNA. This is beyond core values. The embedded core belief helps give an organization a singular focus on something that is key to their short- and longer-term survivability or differentiation.

> *For example—survivability: in a heavy industrial environment, an embedded core belief might be safety. To violate this could mean loss of life.*

For example—differentiation: in a business that is not typically known for honest business dealings, the organization could differentiate themselves with "integrity" as an embedded core belief. To violate this could mean loss of brand image and differentiation in the marketplace.

An embedded core belief is, typically, an area where very little, if any, empowerment is given. You do not consciously violate the embedded core belief and stay with the organization. If this intentionally happens, the disconnect between the organizational beliefs and a chosen personal behavior would be too great.

Empowerment

The term "empowerment" refers to giving people the authority and responsibility to make decisions and take actions. Empowerment results in decisions being made closest to the "front line," where work-related knowledge and understanding reside.

Empowerment is aimed at enabling people to satisfy customers on first contact, to improve processes and increase productivity, and to improve the organization's performance results. An empowered workforce requires information to make appropriate decisions; thus, an organizational requirement is to provide that information in a timely and useful way.

Enterprise Systems Model

The term "Enterprise Systems Model" (ESM) refers to a depiction of the flow of an organization which shows the major systems. These include the "work systems" which refer to how the work of your organization is accomplished (see the definition of "work systems"); the "guidance systems," which refer to how the work of your organization (in your work systems) is directed, led, and managed (see the definition of "guidance systems"; and the "support systems," which refer to how the work of your organization (in your work systems) is supported (see the definition of support systems.)

An Enterprise Systems Model is frequently used to show how the work of the organization is delivered to the external customer, and is led and supported. Typically the listening to the external customer is an input to the guidance systems, which can change how the organization is guided.

An Enterprise Systems Model can be broken down to: 1) individual systems; 2) processes under each of the systems; and 3) one or more levels of sub-processes down to an appropriate level. Each system or process is typically owned by an individual in the organization, who has the responsibility to define, measure, stabilize, and improve it (see the definition of Systematic Process).

Ethical Behavior

The term "ethical behavior" refers to how an organization ensures that all its decisions, actions, and stakeholder interactions conform to the organization's moral and professional principles. These principles should support all applicable laws and regulations and are the foundation for the organization's culture and values. They distinguish "right" from "wrong."

Senior leaders should act as role models for these principles of behavior. The principles apply to all people involved in the organization, from temporary members of the workforce to members of the board of directors. They need to be communicated and reinforced on a regular basis. Although there is no universal model for ethical behavior, senior leaders should ensure that the organization's mission and vision are aligned with its ethical principles. Ethical behavior should be practiced with all stakeholders, including the workforce, shareholders, customers, partners, suppliers, and the organization's local community. While some organizations may view their ethical principles as boundary conditions restricting behavior, well-designed and clearly articulated ethical principles should empower people to make effective decisions with great confidence.

Goals

The term "goals" refers to a future condition or performance level that one intends to attain. Goals can be both short- and longer-term. Goals are ends that guide actions. Quantitative goals, frequently referred to as "targets," include a numerical point or range. Targets might be projections based on comparative or competitive data. The term "stretch goals" refers to desired major, discontinuous (non-incremental) or "breakthrough" improvements, usually in areas most critical to your organization's future success.

Goals can serve many purposes, including:

- Clarifying strategic objectives and action plans to indicate how you will measure success
- Fostering teamwork by focusing on a common end
- Encouraging "out-of-the-box" thinking or innovation to achieve a stretch goal
- Providing a basis for measuring and accelerating progress

Governance

The term "governance" refers to the system of management and controls exercised in the stewardship of your organization. It includes the responsibilities of your organization's owners/shareholders, board of directors, and senior leaders. Corporate or organizational charters, bylaws, and policies document the rights and responsibilities of each of the parties and describe how your organization will be directed and controlled to ensure: (1) accountability to owners/shareholders and other stakeholders, (2) transparency of operations, and (3) fair treatment of all stakeholders. Governance processes may include the approval of strategic direction, the monitoring and evaluation of the CEO's performance, the establishment of executive compensation and benefits, succession planning, financial auditing, risk management, disclosure, and shareholder reporting. Ensuring effective governance is important to stakeholders' and the larger society's trust and to organizational effectiveness.

Guidance Systems

The term "guidance systems" refers to how the work of your organization (in your work systems) is directed, led, and managed. Guidance systems are typically internal to the organization. These systems can include systems for leadership, planning, governance, legal, ethical, community support, and improvement. Guidance systems will direct, lead or manage your workforce, your key suppliers and partners, your contractors, your collaborators, and other components of the supply chain needed to support the work systems which produce and deliver your products and services.

Guidance systems may also be called Management Systems, but are not the same as a Leadership System, which is only one of the Guidance Systems needed.

Health Care Services

All services delivered by your organization that involve professional clinical/medical judgment, including those delivered to patients and to the community. Health care services also include services that are not considered clinical or medical, such as admissions, food services, and billing.

High-Performance

Ever-higher levels of overall organizational and individual performance, including quality, productivity, innovation rate, and cycle time. High performance results in improved service and value for customers and other stakeholders.

Approaches to high performance vary in their form, their function, and the incentive systems used. High performance stems from and enhances workforce engagement. It involves cooperation between the management and the workforce, which may involve workforce bargaining units; cooperation among work units, often involving teams; empowerment of your people, including personal accountability; and workforce input into planning. It may involve learning and building individual and organizational skills; learning from other organizations; creating flexible job design and work assignments; maintaining a flattened organizational structure where decision making is decentralized and decisions are made closest to the front line; and effectively using performance measures, including comparisons. Many organizations encourage high performance with monetary and nonmonetary incentives based on factors such as organizational performance, team and individual contributions, and skill building. Also, approaches to high performance usually seek to align your organization's structure, core competencies, work, jobs, workforce development, and incentives.

How

The term "how" refers to the systems and processes that an organization uses to accomplish its mission requirements. In responding to "how" questions in the Process Item requirements, process descriptions should include information such as approach (methods and measures), deployment, learning, and integration factors. *Responses lacking such information, or merely providing an example, are referred to in the Scoring Guidelines as "anecdotal information."*

Innovation

The term "innovation" refers to making meaningful change to improve products, processes, or organizational effectiveness and to create new value for stakeholders. Innovation involves the adoption of an idea, process, technology, product, or business model that is either new or new to its proposed application. The outcome of innovation is a discontinuous or breakthrough change in results, products, or processes.

Successful organizational innovation is a multistep process that involves development and knowledge sharing, a decision to implement, implementation, evaluation, and learning. Although innovation is often associated with technological innovation, it is applicable to all key organizational processes that would benefit from change, whether through breakthrough improvement or a change in approach or outputs. It could include fundamental changes in organizational structure or the business model to more effectively accomplish the organization's work.

Integration

The term "integration" refers to the harmonization of plans, processes, information, resource decisions, actions, results, and analyses to support key organization-wide goals. Effective integration goes beyond alignment and is achieved when the individual components of a performance management system operate as a fully interconnected unit.

Integration is one of the dimensions considered in evaluating both Process and Results Items. For further description, see the "Scoring System." See also the definition of "alignment."

Intelligent Risks

Opportunities for which the potential gain outweighs the potential harm or loss to your organiza-tion's sustainability if you do not explore them. Taking intelligent risks requires a tolerance for failure and an expectation that innovation is not achieved by initiating only successful endeavors. At the outset, organizations must invest in potential successes while realizing that some will lead to failure.

The degree of risk that is intelligent to take will vary by the pace and level of threat and opportunity in the industry. In a rapidly-changing industry with constant introductions of new products, processes, or business models, there is an obvious need to invest more resources in intelligent risks than in a stable industry. In the latter, organizations must monitor and explore growth potential and change but, most likely, with a less significant commitment of resources. See also "strategic opportunities."

Key

The term "key" refers to the major or most important elements or factors, those that are critical to achieving your intended outcome. The Baldrige Criteria, for example, refers to key challenges, key plans, key work processes, and key measures—those that are most important to your organization's success. They are the essential elements for pursuing or monitoring a desired outcome.

Knowledge Assets

The term "knowledge assets" refers to the accumulated intellectual resources of your organization. It is the knowledge possessed by your organization and its workforce in the form of information, ideas, learning, understanding, memory, insights, cognitive and technical skills, and capabilities. Your workforce, software, patents, databases, documents, guides, policies and procedures, and technical drawings are repositories of your organization's knowledge assets. Knowledge assets are held not only by an organization but reside within its customers, suppliers, and partners, as well.

Knowledge assets are the "know-how" that your organization has available to use, to invest, and to grow. Building and managing its knowledge assets are key components for your organization to create value for your stakeholders and to help sustain a competitive advantage.

Leadership System

The term "leadership system" refers to how leadership is exercised, formally and informally, throughout the organization; it is the basis for and the way key decisions are made, communicated, and carried out. It includes structures and mechanisms for decision making; two-way communication; selection and development of leaders and managers; and reinforcement of values, ethical behavior, directions, and performance expectations.

An effective leadership system respects the capabilities and requirements of workforce members and other stakeholders, and it sets high expectations for performance and performance improvement. It builds loyalties and teamwork based on the organization's vision and values and the pursuit of shared goals. It encourages and supports initiative and appropriate risk taking, subordinates organizational structure to purpose and function, and avoids chains of command that require long decision paths. An effective leadership system includes mechanisms for the leaders to conduct self-examination, receive feedback, and improve.

The term "leader," as it is used in reference to the Leadership System, refers to all leaders at any level in the organization. This is not only limited the top leaders (the head of the organization and that person's direct reports, which are referred to as "Senior Leadership"), but includes every leader supervising at least one other person. In some organizations key positions are considered leaders even if they do not supervise, and in other organizations all employees are considered leaders.

Learning

The term "learning" refers to new knowledge or skills acquired through evaluation, study, experience, and innovation. The Baldrige Criteria includes two distinct kinds of learning: organizational and personal. Organizational learning is achieved through research and development, evaluation and improvement cycles, workforce and stakeholder ideas and input, best-practice sharing, and benchmarking. Personal learning is achieved through education, training, and developmental opportunities that further individual growth.

To be effective, learning should be embedded in the way an organization operates. Learning contributes to a competitive advantage and sustainability for the organization and its workforce. For further description of organizational and personal learning, see the related "Core Value and Concept."

Learning is one of the dimensions considered in evaluating Process Items. For further description, see the "Scoring System."

Levels

The term "levels" refers to numerical information that places or positions an organization's results and performance on a meaningful measurement scale. Performance levels permit evaluation relative to past performance, projections, goals, and appropriate comparisons.

Measures and Indicators

The term "measures and indicators" refers to numerical information that quantifies input, output, and performance dimensions of processes, products, programs, projects, services, and the overall organization (outcomes). Measures and indicators might be simple (derived from one measurement) or composite.

The Criteria does not make a distinction between measures and indicators. However, some users of these terms prefer "indicator" (1) when the measurement relates to performance but is not a direct measure of such performance. For example, the number of complaints is an indicator of dissatisfaction but not a direct measure of it, and (2) when the measurement is a predictor ("leading indicator") of some more significant performance. For example, increased customer satisfaction might be a leading indicator of market share gain.

Mission

The term "mission" refers to the overall function of an organization. The mission answers the question, "What is this organization attempting to accomplish?" The mission might define customers or markets served, distinctive or core competencies, or technologies used.

Multiple Requirements

The term "multiple requirements" refers to the individual questions Criteria users need to answer within each Area to Address. These questions constitute the details of an item's requirements. They are presented in black text under each item's Area(s) to Address.

Overall Requirements

The term "overall requirements" refers to the topics Criteria users need to address when responding to the central theme of an item. Overall requirements address the most significant features of the item requirements. In the Criteria, the overall requirements of each item are presented in one or more introductory sentences printed in bold.

Partners

The term "partners" refers to those key organizations or individuals who are working in concert with your organization to achieve a common goal or to improve performance. Typically, partnerships are formal arrangements for a specific aim or purpose, such as to achieve a strategic objective or to deliver a specific product.

Formal partnerships are usually for an extended period of time and involve a clear understanding of the individual and mutual roles and benefits for the partners. See also the definition of "collaborators."

Patient

The person receiving health care, including preventive, promotional, acute, chronic, rehabilitative, and all other services in the continuum of care. Other terms used for patient include member, consumer, client, and resident.

Performance

The term "performance" refers to outputs and their outcomes obtained from processes, products, and customers that permit evaluation and comparison relative to goals, standards, past results, and other organizations. Performance can be expressed in nonfinancial and financial terms.

The Baldrige Criteria addresses four types of performance: (1) product, (2) customer-focused, (3) financial and marketplace, and (4) operational.

> **"Product performance"** refers to performance relative to measures and indicators of product and service characteristics important to customers. Examples include product reliability, on-time delivery, customer-experienced defect levels, and service response time. For nonprofit organizations, "product performance" examples might include program and project performance in the areas of rapid response to emergencies, at-home services, or multilingual services.

"Customer-focused performance" refers to performance relative to measures and indicators of customers' perceptions, reactions, and behaviors. Examples include customer retention, complaints, and customer survey results.

"Financial and marketplace performance" refers to performance relative to measures of cost, revenue, and market position, including asset utilization, asset growth, and market share. Examples include returns on investments, value added per employee, debt-to-equity ratio, returns on assets, operating margins, performance to budget, the amount in reserve funds, cash-to-cash cycle time, other profitability and liquidity measures, and market gains.

"Operational performance" refers to workforce, leadership, organizational, and ethical performance relative to effectiveness, efficiency, and accountability measures and indicators. Examples include cycle time, productivity, waste reduction, workforce turnover, workforce cross-training rates, regulatory compliance, fiscal accountability, and community involvement. Operational performance might be measured at the work unit level, key work process level, and organizational level.

Performance Excellence

The term "performance excellence" refers to an integrated approach to organizational performance management that results in (1) delivery of ever-improving value to customers and stakeholders, contributing to organizational sustainability; (2) improvement of overall organizational effectiveness and capabilities; and (3) organizational and personal learning. The Baldrige Criteria for Performance Excellence provides a framework and an assessment tool for understanding organizational strengths and opportunities for improvement and thus for guiding planning efforts.

Defining success is a moving target. The definition of success for organizations of all types (profit seeking, nonprofit, and government) is continuously changing and increasingly complex. From the mid-1940s to the 1970s, the limited global competition allowed business leaders in the United States to focus mainly on financial results. The party ended around 1980 when Xerox woke up to a situation where the Japanese were selling copiers in the United States for what it was costing Xerox to make them (Kotter & Heskett, 1992). During the 1980s, quality became a key success factor and was directly linked to market and ultimately financial success. In the beginning, many proposed that high quality was simply too expensive. However, we eventually discovered that high quality equaled reduced cost and increased market share or, as Phillip Crosby wrote in a book by the same title, Quality is Free! *As the service industry and in particular the knowledge worker industries increased in size and importance, they discovered that talented passionate people are also a key to high quality and financial performance. During the 1990s, successful organizations became quite good at "connecting the dots" or as FedEx called it—"people, service, profit" (AMA, 1991). The bar" is being raised once again to include sustainable results in three key areas: financial, environmental, and societal or as Elkington, Emerson, and Beloe (2006) call it—the triple bottom line.*

Performance Projections

The term "performance projections" refers to estimates of future performance. Projections may be inferred from past performance, may be based on competitors' or similar organizations' performance that must be met or exceeded, may be predicted based on changes in a dynamic environment, or may be goals for future performance. Projections integrate estimates of your organization's rate of improvement and change, and they may be used to indicate where breakthrough improvement or innovation is needed. While performance projections may be set to attain a goal, they also may be predicted levels of future performance that indicate the challenges your organization faces in achieving a goal. Thus, performance projections serve as a key management planning tool.

Process

Linked activities with the purpose of producing a product (or service) for a customer (user) within or outside your organization. Generally, processes involve combinations of people, machines, tools, techniques, materials, and improvements in a defined series of steps or actions. Processes rarely operate in isolation and must be considered in relation to other processes that impact them. In some situations, processes might require adherence to a specific sequence of steps, with documentation (sometimes formal) of procedures and requirements, including well-defined measurement and control steps.

In the delivery of services, particularly those that directly involve customers, *process* is used more generally to spell out what delivering that service entails, possibly including a preferred or expected sequence. If a sequence is critical, the process needs to include information that helps customers understand and follow the sequence. Such service processes also require guidance for service providers on handling contingencies related to customers' possible actions or behaviors.

In knowledge work, such as strategic planning, research, development, and analysis, process does not necessarily imply formal sequences of steps. Rather, process implies general understandings of competent performance in such areas as timing, options to include, evaluation, and reporting. Sequences might arise as part of these understandings.

Process is one of the two dimensions evaluated in a Baldrige-based assessment. This evaluation is based on four factors: approach, deployment, learning, and integration. For further description, see the Scoring System.

Productivity

The term "productivity" refers to measures of the efficiency of resource use.

Although the term often is applied to single factors such as the workforce (labor productivity), machines, materials, energy, and capital, the productivity concept applies as well to the total resources used in producing outputs. The use of an aggregate measure of overall productivity allows a determination of whether the net effect of overall changes in a process—possibly involving resource trade-offs—is beneficial.

Purpose

The term "purpose" refers to the fundamental reason that an organization exists. The primary role of purpose is to inspire an organization and guide its setting of values. Purpose is generally broad and enduring. Two organizations in different businesses could have similar purposes, and two organizations in the same business could have different purposes.

RCD

The term "RCD" is a term used for mapping processes. It stands for **Really Crummy Draft**.

If someone is asked to map a process, they will stress out and not deliver the process map in a reasonable (or even over an extended) time. If you tell them, however, "I only need a Really Crummy Draft (RCD)" then they can map a process very quickly. Once the RCD is developed, it can be modified and improved quickly, giving a finished result in less time, and with more participation (and ownership), than if one person was "tasked" to develop a perfect process map.

Results

Outputs and outcomes achieved by your organization in addressing the requirements of a Baldrige Criteria Item. Results are evaluated on the basis of current performance; performance relative to appropriate comparisons; the rate, breadth, and importance of performance improvements; and the relationship of results measures to key organizational performance requirements. Results are on the two dimensions evaluated in a Baldrige-based assessment. This evaluation is based on four factors:

levels, trends, comparisons, and integration. For further description, see the "Scoring System."

Segment

The term "segment" refers to a part of an organization's overall customer, market, product offering, or workforce base. Segments typically have common characteristics that can be grouped logically. In Results Items, the term refers to disaggregating results data in a way that allows for meaningful analysis of an organization's performance. It is up to each organization to determine the specific factors that it uses to segment its customers, markets, products, and workforce.

Understanding segments is critical to identifying the distinct needs and expectations of different customer, market, and workforce groups and to tailoring product offerings to meet their needs and expectations. As an example, market segmentation might be based on distribution channels, business volume, geography, or technologies employed. Workforce segmentation might be based on geography, skills, needs, work assignments, or job classifications.

Senior Leaders

The term "senior leaders" refers to an organization's senior management group or team. In many organizations, this consists of the head of the organization and his or her direct reports.

Stakeholders

The term "stakeholders" refers to all groups that are or might be affected by an organization's actions and success. Examples of key stakeholders might include customers, the workforce, partners, collaborators, governing boards, stockholders, donors, suppliers, taxpayers, regulatory bodies, policy makers, funders, and local and professional communities. See also the definition of "customer."

Strategic Advantages

The term "strategic advantages" refers to those marketplace benefits that exert a decisive influence on an organization's likelihood of future success. These advantages frequently are sources of an organization's current and future competitive success relative to other providers of similar products. Strategic advantages generally arise from either or both of two sources: (1) core competencies, which focus on building and expanding on an organization's internal capabilities, and (2) strategically important external resources, which are shaped and leveraged through key external relationships and partnerships.

When an organization realizes both sources of strategic advantage, it can amplify its unique internal capabilities by capitalizing on complementary capabilities in other organizations.

See the definitions of "strategic challenges" and "strategic objectives" below for the relationship among strategic advantages, strategic challenges, and the strategic objectives an organization articulates to address its challenges and advantages.

Strategic Challenges

The term "strategic challenges" refers to those pressures that exert a decisive influence on an organization's likelihood of future success. These challenges frequently are driven by an organization's future competitive position relative to other providers of similar products. While not exclusively so, strategic challenges generally are externally driven. However, in responding to externally-driven strategic challenges, an organization may face internal strategic challenges.

External strategic challenges may relate to customer or market needs or expectations; product or technological changes; or financial, societal, and other risks or needs. Internal strategic challenges may relate to an organization's capabilities or its human and other resources.

See the definitions of "strategic advantages" and "strategic objectives" for the relationship among strategic challenges, strategic advantages, and the strategic objectives an organization articulates to address its challenges and advantages.

Strategic Objectives

The term "strategic objectives" refers to an organization's articulated aims or responses to address major change or improvement, competitiveness or social issues, and business advantages. Strategic objectives generally are focused both externally and internally and relate to significant customer, market, product, or technological opportunities and challenges (strategic challenges). Broadly stated, they are what an organization must achieve to remain or become competitive and ensure long-term sustainability. Strategic objectives set an organization's longer-term directions and guide resource allocations and redistributions. See the definition of "action plans" for the relationship between strategic objectives and action plans and for an example of each.

Strategic Opportunities

Prospects that arise from outside-the-box thinking, brainstorming, capitalizing on serendipity, research and innovation processes, nonlinear extrapolation of current conditions, and other approaches to imagining a different future.

The generation of ideas that lead to strategic opportunities benefits from an environment that encourages non-directed, free thought. Choosing which strategic opportunities to pursue involves consideration of relative risk, financial and otherwise, and then making intelligent choices (*intelligent risks*).

See action plans for the relationship between strategic objectives and action plans and for an example of each. See also "intelligent risks."

Support Systems

The term "support systems" refers to how the work of your organization in your work systems is supported. Support systems can be internal to the organization or external (such as a corporate HR department providing HR services for a division, or subcontracting your IT). Support systems may involve your workforce, your key suppliers and partners, your contractors, your collaborators, and other components of the supply chain needed to support the work systems which produce and deliver your products and services.

Support systems, by themselves, cannot ensure that an organization is a success. They are critical systems, however, and, if not effectively planned, integrated, and executed, can ensure that the organization fails.

Sustainability

The term "sustainability" refers to your organization's ability to address current business needs and to have the agility and strategic management to prepare successfully for your future business, market, and operating environment. Both external and internal factors need to be considered. The specific combination of factors might include industry-wide and organization-specific components.

Sustainability considerations might include workforce capability and capacity, resource availability, technology, knowledge, core competencies, work systems, facilities, and equipment. Sustainability might be affected by changes in the marketplace and customer preferences, changes in the financial markets, and changes in the legal and regulatory environment. In addition, sustainability has a component related to day-to-day preparedness for real-time or short-term emergencies.

In the context of the Baldrige Criteria, the impact of your organization's products and operations on society and the contributions you make to the well-being of environmental, social, and economic systems are part of your organization's overall societal responsibilities. Whether and how your organization addresses such considerations also may affect its sustainability.

Operational sustainability typically includes the organization verifying that risks associated with money, data, facilities, equipment, workforce, critical skills, and supply chain have been mitigated, or contingency/recovery plans are in place. Strategic sustainability will depend upon these same factors, plus the effectiveness of the strategy and the quality of leadership and leadership development.

According to the Brundtland Commission, "Sustainable development is development that meets the needs of the present without compromising the ability of future generations to meet their own needs."

Systematic

The term "systematic" refers to approaches that are well-ordered, are repeatable, and use data and information so learning is possible. In other words, approaches are systematic if they build in the opportunity for evaluation, improvement, and sharing, thereby permitting a gain in maturity. For use of the term, see the "Scoring Guidelines."

Systematic Process

A systematic process, typically, is a process where the steps undertaken are:

Defined: *how the organization does something. The steps are defined to a level where all parties involved and/or outsiders can understand the sequence of activities, who is involved, and what happens in each step).*

Measured: *each of the steps has measures. These can be in-process measures or end-of-process measures, which indicate whether or not steps and/or the entire process is on track.*

Stabilized: *this means that each step of the process and/or the entire process is reliable or repeatable, and can give consistent results to the organization.*

Improved: *each of the processes has improvement and feedback cycles. Each time you go through the process there is a learning cycle which can be used at the beginning of that process the next time it is repeated.*

Transformational Change

A fundamental shift in the operations, services, or approach of an organization. A transformational change may not require a shift in the mission, vision, or values of an organization, but typically does require a shift in the focus, plans, measures, or behaviors. This shift in the culture of an organization is a result in a change in the strategy and processes that the organization has used in the past. A transformational change is designed to be organization-wide and is enacted over a period of time.

Transparency (from Wikipedia for Corporate Transparency)

Corporate transparency describes the extent to which a corporation's actions are observable by outsiders. This is a consequence of regulation, local norms, and the set of information, privacy, and business policies concerning corporate decision making and operations openness to employees, stakeholders, shareholders, and the general public. From the perspective of outsiders, transparency can be defined simply as the perceived quality of intentionally shared information from the corporation.

Recent research suggests there are three primary dimensions of corporate transparency: information disclosure, clarity, and accuracy. To increment transparency, corporations infuse greater disclosure, clarity, and accuracy into their communications with stakeholders. For example, governance decisions to voluntarily share information related to the firm's ecological impact with environmental activists indicate disclosure; decisions to actively limit the use of technical terminology, fine print, or complicated mathematical notations in the firm's correspondence with suppliers and customers indicate clarity; and decisions to not bias, embellish, or otherwise distort known facts in the firm's communications with investors indicate accuracy. The strategic management of transparency therefore involves intentional modifications in disclosure, clarity, and accuracy to accomplish the firm's objectives.

Trends

The term "trends" refers to numerical information that shows the direction and rate of change for an organization's results. Trends provide a time sequence of organizational performance.

Generally, a minimum of three historical (not projected) data points is needed to begin to ascertain a trend. More data points are needed to define a statistically valid trend. The time period for a trend is determined by the cycle time of the process being measured. Shorter cycle times demand more frequent measurement, while longer cycle times might require longer time periods before meaningful trends can be determined.

Examples of trends called for by the Criteria include data related to product performance, customer and workforce satisfaction and dissatisfaction results, financial performance, marketplace performance, and operational performance, such as cycle time and productivity.

Value

The term "value" refers to the perceived worth of a product, process, asset, or function relative to cost and to possible alternatives.

Organizations frequently use value considerations to determine the benefits of various options relative to their costs, such as the value of various product and service combinations to customers. Organizations need to understand what different stakeholder groups value and then deliver value to each group. This frequently requires balancing value for customers and other stakeholders, such as your workforce and the community.

Values

The term "values" refers to the guiding principles and behaviors that embody how your organization and its people are expected to operate. Values reflect and reinforce the desired culture of an organization. Values support and guide the decision making of every workforce member, helping the organization accomplish its mission and attain its vision in an appropriate manner. Examples of values might include demonstrating integrity and fairness in all interactions, exceeding customer expectations, valuing individuals and diversity, protecting the environment, and striving for performance excellence every day.

Vision

The term "vision" refers to the desired future state of your organization. The vision describes where the organization is headed, what it intends to be, or how it wishes to be perceived in the future.

Voice of the Customer

Your process for capturing customer-related information. Voice-of-the-customer processes are intended to be proactive and continuously innovative to capture stated, unstated, and anticipated customer requirements, expectations, and desires. The goal is to achieve customer engagement. Listening to the voice of the customer might include gathering and integrating various types of customer data, such as survey data, focus group findings, warranty data, and complaint data that affect customers' purchasing and engagement decisions.

Work Processes

The term "work processes" refers to your most important internal value creation processes. They might include product design and delivery, customer support, supply chain management, business, and support processes. They are the processes that involve the majority of your organization's workforce and produce customer, stakeholder, and stockholder value.

Your key work processes frequently relate to your core competencies, to the factors that determine your success relative to competitors, and to the factors considered important for business growth by your senior leaders.

Work Systems

The term "work systems" refers to how the work of your organization is accomplished. Work systems involve your workforce, your key suppliers and partners, your contractors, your collaborators, and other components of the supply chain needed to produce and deliver your products and your business and support processes. Your work systems coordinate the internal work processes and the external resources necessary for you to develop, produce, and deliver your products to your customers and to succeed in your marketplace.

Decisions about work systems are strategic. These decisions involve protecting and capitalizing on core competencies, and deciding what should be procured or produced outside your organization in order to be efficient and sustainable in your marketplace.

Workforce

The term "workforce" refers to all people actively involved in accomplishing the work of your organization, including paid employees (for example, permanent, part-time, temporary, and telecommuting employees, as well as contract employees supervised by the organization) and volunteers, as appropriate. The workforce includes team leaders, supervisors, and managers at all levels.

Workforce Capability

The term "workforce capability" refers to your organization's ability to accomplish its work processes through the knowledge, skills, abilities, and competencies of its people.

Capability may include the ability to build and sustain relationships with your customers; to innovate and transition to new technologies; to develop new products and work processes; and to meet changing business, market, and regulatory demands.

Workforce Capacity

The term "workforce capacity" refers to your organization's ability to ensure sufficient staffing levels to accomplish its work processes and successfully deliver your products to your customers, including the ability to meet seasonal or varying demand levels.

Workforce Engagement

The term "workforce engagement" refers to the extent of workforce commitment, both emotional and intellectual, to accomplishing the work, mission, and vision of the organization. Organizations with high levels of workforce engagement are often characterized by high-performing work environments in which people are motivated to do their utmost for the benefit of their customers and for the success of the organization.

In general, members of the workforce feel engaged when they find personal meaning and motivation in their work and when they receive positive interpersonal and workplace support. An engaged workforce benefits from trusting relationships, a safe and cooperative environment, good communication and information flow, empowerment, and performance accountability. Key factors contributing to engagement include training and career development, effective recognition and reward systems, equal opportunity and fair treatment, and family friendliness.

Index

A

action plans
   implementation of, 53
   modification, 56
   strategic objectives, 53
alignment, 54, 82, 98, 108, 111
Apple Inc., 14
assets, of organization, 6

B

balancing value, 27, 143
Baldrige Criteria for Performance Excellence (CPE) model, xiii
benchmarking, 76, 84
best-practice sharing, 84
big data, 43, 83
blind spots, 46, 107
board of directors, 9
business challenges, 16

C

Canadian Awards for Excellence, xiii
change management, 92
climate change, 23, 106, 118
collaborators, 87, 96, 106–107
Collins, Jim, 14
commercial for-profit organizations, 139
communication
   Criteria For Performance Excellence (CPE), 26–27
   focus on action, 28–29
   and organizational performance, 27–29
community support, 39–40
competition
   competitive advantages, 17
   competitiveness of organization
      changes in, 13–14
      comparative data, 14–15
      Criteria For Performance Excellence (CPE), 11–12
      position of, 12–13
      success factors, 13

competitors
   performance of, 55
   satisfaction relative to, 63
complaint management, 70–71
core competencies, 5, 11, 92, 101, 108–110
   work systems and, 46–47
cost control, 115
Criteria For Performance Excellence (CPE), xv–xvi
   action plan development and deployment, 51–53
   communication and organizational performance, 26–27
   competitiveness of organization, 11–12
   customer
      listening, 57–58
      relationships, 68–69
      satisfaction, 61–62
   customer-focused
      product and process, 121–123
      results, 128
   data, information, and information technology, 85–86
   financial and market results, 137–138
   innovation management, 112
   leadership and governance results, 132–134
   legal and ethical behavior, 33–34
   organizational
      environment, 1–3
      governance, 30–31
      knowledge, 82–83
      relationships, 7–8
   performance
      analysis and review, 78–79
      improvement system, 18
      measurement, 73–74
   process
      efficiency and effectiveness, 114
      management, 109–110
   product
      offerings and customer support, 64–65
      and process design, 105–106
   safety and emergency preparedness, 118

societal responsibilities, 37
strategic objectives, 47–48
strategy
    development, 15–16, 41–44
    implementation, 136
supply-chain management, 116
    results, 126
vision, values, and mission, 21–23
work process effectiveness, 124
workforce
    capability and capacity, 89–91
    climate, 93
    engagement and performance, 95–96
    and leader development, 99–100
customer contact training, 67
customer engagement, 62, 129
    customer relationships, 68–71
    product offerings and customer support, 64–68
customer groups, 13, 17, 59, 66–68
customer life cycle, 59
customer loyalty, 62, 70, 122, 129
customer relationships, 63
    complaint management, 70–71
    Criteria For Performance Excellence (CPE), 68–69
    management of, 70
    senior leaders, role of, 69–70
customer satisfaction, 122–123, 129
    Criteria For Performance Excellence (CPE), 61–62
    determination of, 62–63
    drivers of, 68
    engagement (loyalty) and dissatisfaction, 62–63
    and purchase behavior, 123
    relative to competitors, 63
customer segmentation, 67–68
customer support, 66–67
customer value, 111
customer-focused culture, composition of, 69
customer-focused results
    Criteria For Performance Excellence (CPE), 128
    customer
        engagement, 129
        satisfaction, 129
customers and stakeholders, 9–10
cybersecurity, 86
cycle time, 111, 115, 125

D

data collection, 77
data, information, and information technology
    Criteria For Performance Excellence (CPE), 85–86
    data and
        information availability, 87
        information quality, 86
        information security, 86
    emergency availability, 87
    hardware and software properties, 87
data selection decision, 75
datasets, 43
decision making, 77
dissatisfaction, condition for, 63

E

empowerment, 135
Enterprise Systems Model (ESM). *See* stadium chart
ergonomics audits, 94
ethical behavior, 24, 36
ethics, code of, 135
European Quality Award (EFQM), xiii

F

Federal Aviation Administration (FAA), 6
financial and market results
    Criteria For Performance Excellence (CPE), 137–138
    customer's purchase behavior, 139
    of financial performance, 139
    of marketplace performance, 139
Fortune 100 "high tech" firm, 6

G

governance system, 9, 135

H

health assessments, 94
high-performing organizations, 125, 127
human resources, 103

I

industry business cycles, 45
information
    availability, 87

quality, 86
security, 86
information technology (IT). *See* data, information, and information technology
innovation, 24, 45–46, 66, 77
   Criteria For Performance Excellence (CPE), 112
   as a culture, 113–114
   as a process, 113–114
inspect-in-quality, 115
intelligent risks, 29, 46, 113
IT Disaster Plan, 120

K

Kirkpatrick model, 102
knowledge management, 83–84, 117

L

law and regulation, 135
leadership, 135
   communication with workforce, 28
   ethical behavior, 36
   fiscal accountability, 32
   governance, 30–40
      organizational, 32–33
   legal and regulatory compliance, 35–36
   organizational-level objectives, 29
   performance, 25
      evaluation of, 33
   senior leadership, 21–29
   societal responsibilities, 36–40
   strategic plans, 32
learning
   and development effectiveness, 101–102
   organizational, 24, 25, 84, 101
   personal and workforce, 24
Limited Liability Company, 9
listening, customer
   current customer, 59
   methods of, 68
   potential customers, 60
loyalty, customer, 62, 70, 122, 129

M

Malcolm Baldrige National Quality Improvement Act (1987), xiii

N

National Institute of Standards and Technology (NIST), xiii

"near misses" incidents, 94
nonprofit organizations, 4, 16

O

"on-the-way-to-work" crowd, 9–10
on-time delivery, 122
operational challenges, 16–17
operational effectiveness
   process efficiency and effectiveness, 114–115
   safety and emergency preparedness, 118–120
   supply-chain management, 116–117
organization culture
   characteristics of, 4
   customer-focused, 69
   workforce engagement and performance, 96–97
organizational competencies, 69
organizational environment
   assets, 6
   Criteria For Performance Excellence (CPE), 1–3
   organizational profile, 3–4
   product offerings, 4
   regulatory requirements, 6
   vision and mission, 4–5
   workforce profile, 5–6
organizational governance
   Criteria For Performance Excellence (CPE), 30–31
   governance system, 32
   performance evaluation, 33
organizational knowledge
   Criteria For Performance Excellence (CPE), 82–83
   learning, 84
   management of, 83–84, 117
organizational learning, 25, 84, 101
organizational relationships
   Criteria For Performance Excellence (CPE), 7–8
   customers and stakeholders, 9–10
   governance system, 9
   organizational structure, 9
   suppliers and partners, 10–11
organizational structure, 9
outsourcing, 11

P

performance
   analysis and review of, 77–80
   evaluation, 33

improvement system, 17
  best practices, 81
  continuous improvement and innovation, 82
  Criteria For Performance Excellence (CPE), 18
  features of, 18–19
  future performance, 81
management system, 98
measurement, 14, 54
  agility, 77
  comparative data, 76
  Criteria For Performance Excellence (CPE), 73–74
  customer data, 77
  data selection decision, 75
  projections, 54–55
Plan, Do, Study, Act (PDSA), 18–19
planning cycles
  customer, 45
  market-based, 45
  organization, 45
process efficiency and effectiveness
  cost control, 115
  Criteria For Performance Excellence (CPE), 114
  work process, 125
process management
  Criteria For Performance Excellence (CPE), 109–110
  for implementation of process, 110–111
  for product and process improvement, 111–112
  support processes, 111
Process Owners, 111–112
product and process design
  concept of, 108–109
  Criteria For Performance Excellence (CPE), 105–106
  development of, 106–107
  requirements of, 107–108
  work process, 106
product and process results
  customer-focused, 121–123
  health care criteria, 123
  supply-chain management, 126–127
  work process effectiveness, 123–125
product and service quality, 123
product offerings, 4, 60, 66
Public Law 100–107, xiii
public sector customers, 63
publicly traded corporation, 9

R

regulatory environment, of organization, 6
relationship management, 11, 70
resource allocation, 53–54
role-model performance, 24

S

safety and emergency preparedness
  Criteria For Performance Excellence (CPE), 118
  emergency preparedness, 119–120
  safety issues, 119
safety issues, 94, 119
security audits, 94
senior leadership, 21–29
  communication and organizational performance, 26–29
  role in customer relationships, 69–70
  vision, values, and mission, 21–26
    for creating successful organization, 24–25
    Criteria For Performance Excellence (CPE), 21–23
    legal and ethical behavior, 24
service quality, 125
social media, 59, 63
societal responsibility challenges, 17
societal well-being, 39
society, 136
stadium chart, 108, 110
Statistical Process Control (SPC), 115
strategy development
  business challenges, 16
  competitive advantages, 17
  considerations for, 46
  Criteria For Performance Excellence (CPE), 15–16, 41–44
  innovation, 45–46
  objectives of, 47, 48–50
  operational challenges, 16–17
  process of, 41, 45
  societal responsibility challenges, 17
  work systems and core competencies, 46–47
  workforce challenges, 17
strategy implementation
  action plans, 53
    implementation, 53
    modification, 55–56
  Criteria For Performance Excellence (CPE), 51–53, 136

performance
    measures, 54
    projections, 54–55
    resource allocation, 53–54
    results, 137
    workforce plans, 54
success factors, 13
suppliers and partners, 10–11
supply chain
    Criteria For Performance Excellence (CPE), 116, 126
    management of, 117, 127
    networks, 10–11, 25
systematic processes, 32, 40, 82, 94, 107

T

technology cycles, 45
"triple bottom line," concept of, 38

V

value chain, 10
value creation, 10
vision and mission, of an organization, 4–5

W

warranty costs, 115
web-based technologies, 59
wireless Internet, 10
work process effectiveness
    Criteria For Performance Excellence (CPE), 124
    emergency preparedness, 125
    process effectiveness and efficiency, 125
workforce
    capability and capacity, 91, 132
    career progression, 102–103
    challenges, 17
    change management, 92
    climate (*See* workforce climate)
    Criteria For Performance Excellence (CPE), 89–91
    development, 132
    empowerment, 135
    leader development, 100–103
    learning and development, 100–101
        effectiveness, 101–102
    motivation and career development, 103
    new members, 91–92
    plans, 54
    profile, 5–6
    skills and competencies, 91
    value-added activity, 102
    work accomplishment, 92
workforce climate, 132
    Criteria For Performance Excellence (CPE), 93
    environment, 94
    policies and benefits, 94
workforce engagement and performance, 132
    assessment of, 97
    Criteria For Performance Excellence (CPE), 95–96
    elements of, 97
    indicators of, 97
    logic flow of, 97
    management of, 97–99
    organizational culture, 96–97
workforce-focused results
    Criteria For Performance Excellence (CPE), 130–131
    process performance, 131
    product and service quality, 131
    workforce
        capability and capacity, 132
        climate, 132
        development, 132
        engagement, 132

The Knowledge Center
www.asq.org/knowledge-center

Learn about quality. Apply it. Share it.

ASQ's online Knowledge Center is the place to:

- Stay on top of the latest in quality with Editor's Picks and Hot Topics.
- Search ASQ's collection of articles, books, tools, training, and more.
- Connect with ASQ staff for personalized help hunting down the knowledge you need, the networking opportunities that will keep your career and organization moving forward, and the publishing opportunities that are the best fit for you.

Use the Knowledge Center Search to quickly sort through hundreds of books, articles, and other software-related publications.

www.asq.org/knowledge-center

Ask a Librarian

Did you know?

- The ASQ Quality Information Center contains a wealth of knowledge and information available to ASQ members and non-members

- A librarian is available to answer research requests using ASQ's ever-expanding library of relevant, credible quality resources, including journals, conference proceedings, case studies and Quality Press publications

- ASQ members receive free internal information searches and reduced rates for article purchases

- You can also contact the Quality Information Center to request permission to reuse or reprint ASQ copyrighted material, including journal articles and book excerpts

- For more information or to submit a question, visit **http://asq.org/knowledge-center/ask-a-librarian-index**

Visit www.asq.org/qic for more information.

TRAINING CERTIFICATION CONFERENCES MEMBERSHIP **PUBLICATIONS**

The Global Voice of Quality®

Belong to the Quality Community!

Established in 1946, ASQ is a global community of quality experts in all fields and industries. ASQ is dedicated to the promotion and advancement of quality tools, principles, and practices in the workplace and in the community.

The Society also serves as an advocate for quality. Its members have informed and advised the U.S. Congress, government agencies, state legislatures, and other groups and individuals worldwide on quality-related topics.

Vision

By making quality a global priority, an organizational imperative, and a personal ethic, ASQ becomes the community of choice for everyone who seeks quality technology, concepts, or tools to improve themselves and their world.

ASQ is...

- More than 90,000 individuals and 700 companies in more than 100 countries

- The world's largest organization dedicated to promoting quality

- A community of professionals striving to bring quality to their work and their lives

- The administrator of the Malcolm Baldrige National Quality Award

- A supporter of quality in all sectors including manufacturing, service, healthcare, government, and education

- YOU

Visit www.asq.org for more information.

TRAINING CERTIFICATION CONFERENCES MEMBERSHIP **PUBLICATIONS**   The Global Voice of Quality®

ASQ Membership

Research shows that people who join associations experience increased job satisfaction, earn more, and are generally happier*. ASQ membership can help you achieve this while providing the tools you need to be successful in your industry and to distinguish yourself from your competition. So why wouldn't you want to be a part of ASQ?

Networking

Have the opportunity to meet, communicate, and collaborate with your peers within the quality community through conferences and local ASQ section meetings, ASQ forums or divisions, ASQ Communities of Quality discussion boards, and more.

Professional Development

Access a wide variety of professional development tools such as books, training, and certifications at a discounted price. Also, ASQ certifications and the ASQ Career Center help enhance your quality knowledge and take your career to the next level.

Solutions

Find answers to all your quality problems, big and small, with ASQ's Knowledge Center, mentoring program, various e-newsletters, *Quality Progress* magazine, and industry-specific products.

Access to Information

Learn classic and current quality principles and theories in ASQ's Quality Information Center (QIC), *ASQ Weekly* e-newsletter, and product offerings.

Advocacy Programs

ASQ helps create a better community, government, and world through initiatives that include social responsibility, Washington advocacy, and Community Good Works.

Visit www.asq.org/membership for more information on ASQ membership.

*2008, The William E. Smith Institute for Association Research

TRAINING CERTIFICATION CONFERENCES **MEMBERSHIP PUBLICATIONS**